THE DEFINITION OF MAN

A REFLECTION OF SELF

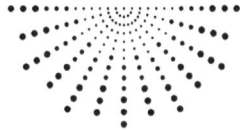

YANCEY MIX

DETROIT INK PUBLISHING

Table of
Contents

DEDICATION

I want to dedicate this to my late mother Gwendolyn Mix who showed me what it was like to overcome hardships and never give up on yourself. She is the reason why I have never given up even when I felt like I wanted to. No matter what highs or lows you may encounter, stay strong in your spirituality and you can get through anything. She showed me what perseverance, strength, dedication, and hope was. Because of my mom, I realized what it was like to have unconditional love for someone rather than judge them based on their mistakes but what's in their heart. Love them because you truly want to see them succeed and want what's best for them and always have their back. She showed me how to treat people with respect no matter what their circumstances may be. She was always the biggest cheerleader for her loved ones. She made sure you knew she was there to cheer you on no matter where she was in the building and always lighting up a room with her contagious smile. I thank her for being the best mother and grandmother she could possibly be regardless of the circumstances. She always made sure her family felt loved. You will always be loved and missed forever mom.

ACKNOWLEDGMENTS

First and foremost I want to thank God for the opportunity to be heard and trusting me enough with a vision that I didn't know I was capable of handling. I want to thank him for making me a natural born leader and not a follower and giving me something to believe in when I felt all hope was lost. Also, for never giving up on me when I felt I wasn't worthy of his forgiveness but still blessing me with the wisdom, knowledge, the mindset and words to complete a project like this. He has placed the right people in my life to help shape and mold me to who I am today. Without him none of this is possible.

I would like to acknowledge some significant people who has always had my back and encouraged me. To Krystle Williams, someone who has helped me along the way and stuck with me through thick and thin. She never gave up on me. I couldn't be more thankful for that. She taught me what love was, the strength of it and how to love. She showed me that it was more than just a physical connection to a woman but that it consisted of intimacy. She always pushed me to want more, try harder, and reach higher than I ever thought I could. She taught me how to set goals, have a vision and believe in myself more than I ever have. She believed in me even when I didn't believe in myself. She helped me get to a position of realizing that life was bigger than me. Understanding life was always in me, but she helped to bring it out like strong women do. I don't know where I would be without her. I probably would still be chasing my tail. She has been one of the most influential, loving, caring, compassionate people I have ever met and I'm glad that she has been a part of my life.

I would also like to acknowledge my kids, Kenede, Kamryn, Kortlan, and Kingston Mix, who give me every reason to breathe, live, and continue on every day. They bring joy and happiness to my life. They are my drive and motivation to build a legacy that will carry on for generations that will make them proud to call me their dad. They are the reason I want to succeed in life. I didn't know what failure was until I felt like I was failing them as a father so it made me step my game up and do everything in my power to change the narrative.

I can't forget my oldest sister Adele Stallworth, or "Momma Dale" as everyone calls her, who has always had my back and gotten me out of jams. I probably wouldn't have been able to get out of them myself. She could've told me "no" plenty of times, but she never did because she knew I needed the help, guidance, or advice. I didn't always listen but she still gave it knowing that one day I would get it. She never judged me or made me feel like I owed her something even though I did. That meant the world to me because I knew she did it out of love. I owe her the world for always being in my corner no matter what and being a motherly big sister when I needed that.

I don't want to leave anyone out so I want to thank all my family and friends who have shown me love, given me wisdom, made me a better person, had my back, and been in my corner when I wasn't deserving of that. Without you there is no me. To the strong sisters and brothers out there who do everything they can to make life easier for the next generation and their loved ones. I salute you too because not everybody has that. Everyone isn't willing to step up and make a difference in someone else's life because they're too busy putting their own selfish ways before the need of others. We need more people like you that cares enough to be role models and leaders. Continue to be a difference maker because you are impacting the world one person at a time.

I also have to acknowledge my editor Pamela Hilliard Owens and her team for helping to make my vision come to light. She has helped me, guided me, and given me the tools necessary to make this a reality. I was blessed to have found her. I know I probably wasn't the easiest to work with but she was patient with me and made it an easy process to publish my first book and make me an author.

INTRODUCTION

I would like to start by looking at the way the world is and the problems that exist within it. Try to figure out the core of the issues and see if I can unravel them and lay them out in front of you so we can dissect them. Pinpoint the common denominator and assist by giving the tools necessary to adjust one's self to be the best possible them. You have to be willing to reflect and know where and how to make life adjustments.

I want to break down the problems with the world so that I can determine how we got to this state of disarray. We have people who don't make family a priority and whole families who don't stay together. We have crime at an all-time high. We have increasingly higher numbers of sexual immorality. We have kids being molested right under our noses in their own homes and family members' homes, both by strangers and even their own family members.

Young men are dropping out of school at an alarming rate. Kids are dealing with drugs at a young age in some form or fashion with disregard to the consequences. Men are going to jail left and right. Men are being killed at a young age. People are not respecting their fellow man. Women are having to work extra hard to pick up the slack for the missing fathers. The list of grievances just goes on.

I'm sure I can't fix all the world's issues, but I do believe I can help contribute something towards a solution. That's through my ability to express myself through writing and understanding of people and how to reach out and relate to them, whoever it may be.

My approach will not be like most but one of laying out the problem, how it has affected society and the individual, and what we can do to turn that same problem around with the right approach. What I want to do is give a different perspective of the problems.

Not from a person who's just telling another person what they need to do differently or a "do as I do "standpoint, but from a perspective of the mind of the person who gets caught up in certain patterns that lead to dysfunctional behaviors. It allows the reader to envision themselves in the character or see characteristics of what I'm describing as if I were holding up a mirror so they may see themselves with conviction and correction. The reason I'm doing that is because I feel if you understand the problem from a little deeper level then it will make for a different approach towards the problem or for a better solution.

I am a person who can relate to just about anybody because of what I've had to endure as a child coming up. I was raised around many negative influences including drugs, alcoholism, abuse, poverty, ghettos, missing parents, molestation, constant moving, and a broken family and I've seen the long-term effect it had on kids as they grew up.

The one constant I noticed through all of it was the lack of role models present to prevent these sorts of things from happening or to help people get back on track when these things do happen. I've also been around positive family environments that had all the male role models present as a foundation to create a better structure from childhood through adulthood and seen the difference that it can make in a child's life. So I guess you can say I'm from both sides of the fence.

I've had a lot to get past and overcome (and am still overcoming) and perhaps you did too. I didn't let it determine my importance as a man, as a father, or as a human being. Nor did I let it dictate the outcome of my life but it's when I decided it wasn't. What I did to keep from being a statistic was use the negative experiences to create positive outcomes because I knew how the negative could affect a child's mental state. It could leave that child feeling unloved, unwanted and with a sense of abandonment or hopeless about life. Everybody isn't able to recycle the negative and turn it into a positive, but I used my childhood as an example of what I didn't want in my future or in my children's future.

According to the National Family Resiliency Center, the problems could have something to do with the 20 million children living in a single parent household or the 24 million children that aren't living in the house with their biological fathers. To me those numbers speak volumes to the link that is missing in the chain. Where are the fathers, the leaders, the teachers, the visionaries, the providers? The ones who are leading the kids by the hand through the walks of life, the ones teaching the kids what to do and what not to do in life. The ones providing what the kids need so they don't have to go out and try and get it on their own without knowing how.

Where is the visionary that understands why you need to pursue your vision as a man? I believe those people are out there just waiting for someone to reach out to them in a way that's relevant to them and they can relate to, so I thought of writing a more relatable book. A book that speaks to the soul of a person not over their heads. One that speaks undeniable truth. A book doesn't have to have a certain face, a certain name or a speaking voice. All it needs is the right words, and I've always been able to come up with right words verbally but never knew if it could translate into a manuscript. I only thought people who were known as writers in some way or another were capable of putting out a book. I never considered myself a writer so the thought never crossed my mind.

I want to speak directly to the men, but if I'm going to do that let me find out what a man is because you should never speak to someone in-depth about a possibly sensitive subject unless you know who they are or what they are made up of. It lowers your chances to offend someone or trigger something that you didn't know was there due to the subject content. So I decided to look up the term "man" in the dictionary.

I always hear about what a man should be, what a man should do, what a man should say, or what a man should look like, but nothing that showed me the content of what a man is made up of. To my surprise there wasn't a definition that I could locate that told me what a man is or at least what I was expecting to see. So I decided to define it for myself before addressing men or males. Now I know what people are going to think or say, what makes me qualified to tell another person what a man is and what I say to that is your right.

I don't feel I'm qualified to tell anybody else what a man is because I haven't always displayed the qualities to call myself the real man that I'm writing about but it took me to understand that and admit to the fact that I was falling short of that goal too. Also what I realized is even though I might not have the credentials of certain professionals or the stature of celebrity status, I understand what I lacked as a man or what I missed out on as a youth once I became a parent. I feel that the natural instincts of parenthood and understanding of life and myself allows me to speak on the subject.

But if you think about it, the difference between the professionals and me is that they studied books that were written by doing research and studies on people's lives that landed them a degree in the field. What wisdom and knowledge are the study of life with its share of research done by reading, viewing and evaluating certain things based on outcomes of paths traveled and I've done my share of that. It also took me to grow as a person and a man mentally and seek the knowledge necessary to get me headed in the right direction because the last thing I wanted to do is be looked at as a hypocrite.

It took for me to open my ears and hear and listen to what others were telling me about myself before I could even feel comfortable enough to approach the subject. I won't sit here and say be like me because I do understand the growth process of a male and that it takes time, maturity mentally and spiritually and a willingness to grow. But what I can do is attempt to provide the necessary tools so that you can reflect on your own life and see if you are you doing the things necessary to accelerate that process and possibly provoke change within yourself if need be.

My definition of man is what you become after you have matured from a young male to an adult. It's not just based on age, height, facial hair, muscles, voice, strength, or genital growth. Nor is it just about who you can beat up, kill or have sex with either. It also has nothing to do with having your own car, place, child or how much money you have. It's a combination of things to complete manhood not one individual claim to fame.

Manhood is based on how you are publicly, including how you conduct yourself around others and how you handle yourself privately behind closed doors. Your public persona can't be totally different than your "at home" demeanor. You should be consistent in who you are at all times in order to avoid being labeled as "fake" or hypocrite. It also means being responsible financially, living within your means and being able to support yourself and others. You have to be able provide a lifestyle that conducive to the growth, safety, and security of you and your family.

Respect is a major factor, respecting yourself and your surroundings whether we mean males or females or the environment in general. Mentally you need be strong and have the mental capacity to handle the stress that comes with being a leader or the head of a household or the head of anything. You can't crack under pressure every time an obstacle comes your way. You have to be able to absorb it, stand strong and move forward when something doesn't go as planned.

When it comes to acting sexually, that should be a selfless act not a selfish one. It is not thinking selfishly about what can be done for you but wanting to please your mate. There should be joy in pleasing the person that you say you care for. If you respect them enough then you won't think twice about doing what you can to put a smile on your mate's face. Now let's not forget this isn't meant for any and everybody but for two people who say they love each other and understand exactly what love is. It's meant for a long-term companionship not a fly-by-night relationship. It's also being capable of becoming that leader whether it's head of a household, group or country.

When you have achieved all the necessary things then you can be labeled not just a man but also a real man, an authentic man, because many times men give themselves this title prematurely. Presently, there's not much to teach people what a real man should be. There's not much that young men are willing to pick up to show them how to be accountable for their actions or how to stand-up strong in the face of adversity and overcome obstacles. Or that shows him how he should be a pillar in the home and the community so that it thrives; how not to be a coward and run from responsibility but handle it to the best of his ability. Who is to show the young ladies who never had a man or male role model the kind of love and respect they should be receiving from a man or what kind of man they should have in their life?

That's what I hope to do with this book: to show the daughter how to have a better picture of what a man should consist of so she doesn't fall victim to the false images or the definition given to her by the males trying to convince her that they're men. How to give the son a better picture of manhood so he can look in the mirror at himself and see if he fits the bill or at least give him a goal to shoot for or make sure he's not too far of course. Hopefully it breeds a better crop of men for women to choose from so there is a good man for every good woman. Now I know that's a stretch but hopefully it narrows the gap.

My goal is to have this book sit in every household, on every shelf, on every desktop or any place there is access to books. Maybe my book can also help the ones who have gotten so far lost in life without a clue on how to get back or where they might of went wrong so it may guide them back on the right path. The book is also for the single parents who can give it to their son(s) or daughter(s) to read and help give them a better understanding of these concepts at an earlier age. Maybe it encourages the son to see past the outside images being fed to him by the cruel eyes of the world through different media outlets and maybe even his own neighborhood. Hopefully the book will exist alongside of the existing mother and/or father's teachings so when the young man finally pokes his chest out and says, "I'm a man," he can do that with confidence and conviction.

What I want to do is give you some different scenarios or short stories that all have the same pattern, but different routes that life can go when there's no father present to balance out the child's upbringing. It has adverse effects on the chemical balance in a child's brain, which is given to them at the time of conception through the genetics of both the mother and the father. Without the balance of both parents in a single generation can lead to generational problems and a lot of bad decision-making among the children caught in that cycle. It takes something out of the equation that is important for the raising of the next generation if there is no role model to step in and fill that void.

As an example you have a mother attempting to raise a boy on her own after she and the father decide to go their separate ways. But the father decides not to play his role after the split. It puts the mom in a bad predicament to either pay more attention to the bills and their living situation or to her son. Since she refused to let them be in the poor house, the bills became the biggest priority, which made it harder to find a balance with raising the son. She had to work long hours or sometimes two jobs to stay ahead. It gave her son an open window to be influenced by the wrong things and to make bad decisions along the way all because he got lost in way of thinking and had no role model to steer him correctly.

Because he wanted life to be different or to change his circumstances although he had limited options to change them, the streets were the only thing around him that seemed to change fortune. He had so many questions but not enough answers and no one he felt comfortable enough to ask. He eventually gets caught up and starts dealing in drugs and that's when things got out of control for him. He has a baby in the mist of it all. He goes to jail a few times with last one costing him some years of his life.

Fortunately, prison did help rehabilitate him and turn his life around but only after meeting some men/mentors in there that help fill him with knowledge and wisdom. He developed a plan so when he got out, he can try to make a positive contribution to society. He gained some skills in carpentry and electrician while being locked up. Once he got out, he continued to pursue it and became a certified electrician and carpenter and eventually started his own business.

Now it was not easy by any stretch of the imagine and it took a while for that to happen because of the number of doors that were closed in his face, but he

wanted the change bad enough to stay persistent. It got so bad that the cycle almost continued by reverting back to what he knew, but he realized that he had to make a change in order to stay out of prison and be a part of his family's life.

I know it is rare for things to work in such a positive fashion exactly the way they are planned, but when you have the mindset to make a change in your life and change your circumstances anything is possible. Your chances to turn things around when you build your credentials and position yourself greatly increase. God always gives us the freedom to choose in our life. When you come to that fork in the road, you can either take the high road, or the low road, but whatever you decide, you will have to live with the consequences of that choice. That road you take is going to shape the outcome of your life, so never forget the path you chose because it ends in either success or chaos.

Like I said, you have to be strong-willed and be willing to change.

Everybody's mind can't recover from turmoil and chaos or it's a lot harder to do so. Luckily in this case scenario or example young man wasn't too far lost mentally or hadn't become institutionalized, which could've made him want to live a life of crime because he felt that's all he had or knew. He wasn't ready to give up on life and accept the way it was. Plus, somebody came into his life that helped him mature and grow which he really hadn't had before.

That's usually the case in a chaotic situation. There's a lack of what's needed. A lot of times the turmoil and chaos cuts so deep and is so far imbedded into the psyche that a person's mind can't wrap itself around the present circumstances being any different than it had been for the majority of their life. It makes it harder to do anything different than what they know.

This situation could've gone like a lot of situations go when a father isn't around and a child gets caught up in the street life. The child feels so abandoned that they stop caring about what life has to offer because they feel they were dealt a bad hand. They also feel no one cares about them and they get knee deep in the street life because it's right at their fingertips and very influential. Sometimes people don't understand the power of environment. It can make them feel important cause they can get the love and attention from the street life and homeboys that they weren't getting from home. They do whatever it takes to get attention, gain the respect and earn stripes towards what they think is manhood. Along the way they never learn the value of a life or a dollar.

What people don't realize until it's too late is the streets don't have no love for you. There's really not a respect factor when it comes to that kind of life and there's a lot of people in it who could care less about the value of a dollar or a person. It's a dog eat dog world. They learn the rules of the street and miss the lessons at home and that's how they live their life. They spend their teenage, young adult, and adult years in and out of jail because of their irresponsible actions and decisions. Technically they become a career criminal until they get killed or caught for a major crime and spend the majority or rest of their life behind bars.

This is just one scenario that could happen or does happen but there are so many more stories that send people on the path of destruction or a lifetime of confusion. What about that kid whose parent(s) is on drugs because that's their way to cope with life? It leaves the child with no supervision or love at home because his or her parent is busy chasing the high and makes that the number one priority. They grow numb or cold because they have to deal with the reality that it's their parent that is known in the neighborhood as a drug addict.

Of course, it makes them shameful because they can't do anything about it but endure the chatter. They have little to nothing because of the living conditions or circumstances. It forces them to do what they have to in order to survive and make something out nothing. The likelihood of them dropping out of school increases by a great percentage because they'll rather be out making money to help their cause as a short-term solution rather than getting an education, which is the long-term solution. Because they are misguided and misdirected, they end up making a lifetime of bad decisions that are hard to bounce back from.

What about that child who gets molested or raped by a stranger or a relative or a parent's partner from a new relationship? Technically, they can be a stranger because you're pretty much moving in with a person that you barely no anything about or at least enough about to ensure the safety of your children around them. But even a relative could cause the same harm so before you release your kids to anyone's else's care besides your own, you have to know that they have the same standards and love for your kids as you do. You have to know that they will go to the same length as you to keep your kids out of harm's way. If you're leaving your children in the care of someone else and you don't have that secure or comfortable feeling as you're walking away, you should not do it.

If your child ever comes to you and says that something happened that made them feel uncomfortable while being with that person(s) don't just ignore them or tell them they're lying for the sake of the relationship. Find out exactly what happened and why they felt that way and address the situation accordingly. See to it that they won't have to be put in that type of situation again because if someone sees that you don't care or that you are not listening to what your child has to say I can ensure you that it will continue and get worse.

God forbid the worst-case scenario does happen like molestation or rape, then the child grows up confused on why that happen or why that was allowed. They sometimes blame themselves, the parent or any loved one that wasn't there to protect them. It can either cause one of two things to happen; the child can either be drawn towards the act of sex or gender or pushed away from the act or gender.

They see the act or gender as a threat or harmful and wants to avoid it or them as much as possible because of the terror and pain and confusion it caused them as a child, so they develop insecurities. Or they're drawn to it possibly because it went on for so long that they start to look at themselves only as a sex tool or object for that gender because they felt used as one for so long. Something like that occasionally causes lesbianism, homosexuality, strippers, or prostitutes as a result because of the mental confusion and the perverse thoughts or actions that are thrust upon them at an early age.

Do you see the parallels in those kinds of lifestyles with the perverse acts forced upon a child? Coincidence, I think not. Now I know that's not the only reason for those types of acts, but some definitely stems from that. It blurs to many lines in an adolescent's mind who can't comprehend what happen to them.

What about that child that grows up in foster care because their parent gave them up for adoption and is constantly moving from family to family feeling unloved and unwanted and tossed around like a piece of trash? They put up a wall because of the lack of trust they develop with anyone along the way. They develop a demeanor of trust issues and feels like it doesn't matter what they do because they're just going to be sent to another family anyway, so life becomes less important to them.

When kids go through these types of events and there is no family that steps up or is able to, then family becomes less of a priority to the scared child. Their view becomes skewered of what family is or does for one another. Not unless they're placed into a home where the adopting family really cares and wants to love you and see you do good in life but how many times do you see that happen. Sometimes people foster children to get a check that's associated with fostering a child instead doing it out of love, so that's why you see foster kids often behave or act out the way they do because its apparent when love isn't present.

So many times in life people grow up thinking that there's nothing wrong with their life or at least try to convince themselves that it's nothing wrong and struggle with issues that lay dormant or gets pushed to the back of their mind because of some things that happened throughout their childhood that never gets resolved.

Bruce Lee once said, "Until you realize you're walking in the darkness, you'll never seek the light," which is so true because if everything always looks dark, grim and negative you will know nothing else. That seems normal to you. How will you ever move towards anything positive if it's unfamiliar territory?

Most people have a fear of the unknown. The truth of your reality can be so much different than the truth of life. That can be a tale of two different stories. Which one are you living? What I mean by that is your reality can be shaped by your circumstance or perspective which can limit your scope or vantage point of what you're capable of. That can be very different from what life really has to offer when you broaden your horizons and understand that you can expand your growth outside the box you feel you're trapped in.

It can dictate how you live and grow up and affect future relationships because of being emotionally closed. Some say it is what it is and just accept life how it is and see no reason to change anything. Their perception of reality gets so misconstrued in their head that it becomes a Picasso painting in their mind, and nothing ever looks normal to them again.

Some kids have parents who deal with depression of their own so the children never get the needed attention, love, and lessons from their parents or the child whose parent(s) suffers from alcoholism or whose parent(s) is a workaholic. Really there are just so many stories and scenarios I could talk about, but you would have had to walked in that person's shoes or told their story to understand fully why they are the way they are. But do know this, there is a reason for a person to think a certain way that may be counterproductive. I can assure you of that and that lack of structure, leaders, role models and mentors that reside in the home is key and vital to the kids who grow up without it.

Fathers: if no one else says it, if no one else believes, I believe in us. I truly believe in my heart that we have what it takes to transform our homes, our community, and a nation as a whole back to the way it was meant to be. Back to a structured manner with the fathers at the helm because that's where we were meant to be. We are the backbone to society. Without us doing our part those things can't stand-up and rise because a body can't stand-up without a strong backbone. With a weakened vertebra it will try to, but it will essentially just fall right back down to the ground and pretty much collapse or crumble exactly the way society is doing.

As men, let's stand-up and stand for something and start building our legacies now, so our kids can have something positive to be proud of. They can have daddies who can come to career day for a change. We want to have something that we can pass down to them besides debt and chaos. They can't do it without us men, no matter what anybody says, it just can't happen.

CHAPTER ONE

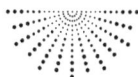

D EFINE YOURSELF

IN ORDER TO DEFINE YOURSELF, you have to know what you want, where you're trying to go, and what's the best route to get there. You have to learn your strengths and weaknesses so you can know how to play them to your advantage. By figuring out what you want life to look like, the easier it is to build a strategy for the long-term.

First, I believe that if the man and woman take care of themselves as individuals before they come together to create a family, it makes for a good foundation for the next generation. Learn to be comfortable in your own skin and with yourself so that you don't succumb to others' influence over your life. Know who you are before you walk out into the world. Be a man who has a vision for yourself, your family, and a strong sense of self. Have an idea of what you want out of life. An idea of where you're trying to go and what it takes to get there. It helps when a person gets a good education first so it can help open up doors in the future. When your grades are good, it allows certain doors to be open that might not be otherwise and place you in positions to be in or around certain environments that can catapult you to that next level. Education is something that should be taken seriously from the start of school. Now I'm not saying that is the only way to become successful or chase and achieve your dreams, but what an education does is make the world around you take you a little more seriously. It shows that you have the ability to pursue and conquer a goal. It also shows you have the ability finish something that you start. It shows that you have the advanced knowledge in a specific field of study so you can perform your job at a high level.

You should explore your physical talents as a child and young adult. Try different things so you can find out what you're passionate about so maybe it becomes more than just a hobby but a career. Passion is something that you love doing whether you're making a lot of money or not. You have the drive to continuously pursue it because you feel you can be successful at it. Parents make sure you're exposing your child to different things so he/she has a better opportunity to find that talent or passion. You might find out that they're good at something that you never would've imagined. And know this; just because you have a God given gift or talent it won't manifest itself. You have to work hard to become the best you can be at it. Whether you're pushing yourself or you have someone guiding you, it just doesn't happen on its own. You know how many talented people never capitalized on their talents. Don't be that person.

You should figure out who you are first. Your likes and dislikes. What kind of life you want to live while you're still young and the complications of adulthood come in to play? Things that make decisions a little harder to make like having kids. The reason I say kids complicate life decisions is because once you have them you should be making decisions based on what's best for that child and yourself not just yourself. You have to support that child by any means necessary and that usually is with a job that isn't considered a career for you because you chose to do things out of order. Once you start working that job you may get complacent with it and forget about the career path or life path you wanted for yourself.

Unfortunately, that job may become boring to you or you may get unhappy with it and the next thing you know time has flown by, and then you feel like it's too late to pursue a dream (although it's never too late). It's better if you make that life decision about what you want to do as a career early on so you can live that life you always wanted without feeling like you missed out on something after the fact. Why wait until you have made a family then decide to pursue things that should've been conquered already? Accomplish your goals first so that it decreases the chances for either parent that thinks about leaving to pursue something else or feel like they didn't get what they wanted out of life. Establish yourself before you get to this point.

The kids need both parents there raising them properly to take away from the major problems that affect a household and society. A man should take the proper route of establishing himself first with some sort of steady income so he can grow and build something that is preparing for a potential family. It should be something that won't have a negative impact on him or anybody close to him. If you're making money but it's putting you or your family at risk, then you're doing more harm than good. If you're chancing not being around for your family, then what's the point?

When you are established and ready to marry, make sure you're evaluating in totality about the person you want to have in your life before you put all your eggs in the basket. See if your likes and dislikes are similar. See what different tastes in food you have, appearance, humor, personal goals, family goals, and how you go about reaching those goals. Find out each other's habits, sexual habits, hobbies, what you consider fun, your pet peeves, etc... Discuss each other's family history at least back to the grandparents so you can know if there's a pattern either good or bad that a person might be following.

It shows you if your productive mate might be family oriented or not. It also helps show you where they are mentally and what kind of effect their childhood could have had on their adulthood. Get to know your mate as if you were trying to get to know yourself. Love yourself so that you can love them the way you would want to be loved. You should want what's best for them. Just make sure you are on the same page and see eye to eye about how you want to approach marriage, parenthood, goals and just life in general.

Once it's done in that order, you're more focused on being a good provider, husband and parent and not playing catch up your whole life; so chose a mate wisely.

CHAPTER TWO

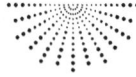

D EFINE YOUR FINANCIAL FUTURE

DEFINING your financial future is understanding how important having your financial affairs in order are. It dictates what you can or can't do. It shifts what you're focused on while trying to establish yourself. You have to understand it can make or break your goals and relationships. You also need to recognize that you have to be prepared financially for each step of life in order to achieve maximum success. You have to budget out your finances accordingly. It is part of life's check and balances.

Once you have established your individual selves then you can establish a life together so there's a stable foundation for the new generation to come into the world and have stability. Make it as easy on them as possible so there are fewer worries in their lives. Prepare for the financial responsibility it's going to take to raise a family by saving in advance. Think about all the males who grow up in a broken home with one parent where rules and money are scarce. One parent is having to work a lot harder to compensate for the lack of money and doesn't have the time to give or doesn't feel up to giving as much attention to the child(s) that is needed so the ripple effects start from there. As a result the child, doesn't get the basic valuable elements from the only parent they have there to teach them on a regular basis.

What does the male instinct do when money is scarce? Try to become a provider even if he isn't quite capable. He goes out and tries to obtain the financial means that would help support his parent (whether legally or illegally) so they don't have to carry the burden alone. To me that isn't a bad thought process because at least he wants to contribute; he just doesn't know a better way to do so or in the position to. He also lacks the basic rules in his decision-making processes. For instance, when he sees a regular job isn't bringing in enough money to ease his mother's sorrows or burdens, he tries another avenue. One that brings the money in a little faster so he can put a temporary smile on her face when he helps out, but he'd rather see her smile all the time. It's usually fast money or hustle money he turns to, but he doesn't think about the disrespectful manner in which he gets money because all he knows is, he's making his household a little better. He's not thinking about what he's doing to anybody else's situation or if he's destroying another family's hopes and dreams. He just knows his isn't as bad as it was, but that's the selfish way of thinking.

That's when his male ego kicks in and he starts feeling manly or macho because of his contribution to his home. Don't let him start getting a little attention from his peers and especially from the opposite sex then he tries to do more of it. I like to use a saying, "all attention isn't good attention" because while fast money might get you a lot more attention just know most of the attention doesn't have good intentions.

Most of the women who are looking at him are looking for an easy route to obtain the financial dollars that he's achieved. They do that by either sleeping with him to keep him close by or by seeing how they can get close enough to set him up. As for the guys who are looking, they are just plotting on the quickest, and way to take it. The crab in a bucket mentality kicks in and someone doesn't want to see the next person doing more than them so they start doing their best to pull you back down.

He normally attracts women who come from similar dysfunctional backgrounds and don't respect themselves or others. She usually looks for a mate with a shallow definition of what a man is. So with that lack of knowledge of the basic rules she gets disrespected but thinks its ok. She doesn't realize it's not ok and it starts a vicious cycle of disrespect or lack of respect that affects their lives and the lives of any future kids.

Together they wouldn't have what it took to instill the proper elements into a child so it would have had minimal chances to succeed in life. All that from the result of a child who just wanted to help ease the stress and burden of money but went about the business of life wrong and ended up with women who was on a similar path that lacked morals and values also. If getting money comes before your family, then you have an addiction the same way a drug addict puts their addiction before their family. It's a cycle that doesn't end until parents who chose not to be there for their child finally realize they are the key to change.

Why do you think people like to say that money is the root of evil? That's because in man's quest to achieve a certain financial status they tend to have clouded vision and sometimes step on whomever it takes to reach that level. If you look back in history and view the negative or illegal things that have occurred, money usually is at the root of the actions. Countries go to war and kill and degrade people over money, so it's been going on for centuries. It gives money an evil persona but really, it's the people attached to it who value money over people that makes that saying relevant. Since currency has been in circulation it has formed a greed within human beings that seems to never get satisfied.

The saying goes, the more money you have, the more power and respect you get so there has always been an attempt to get more and more and it shows in the expansion of the world. People have murdered, stolen, captured, enslaved, and suppressed others just to get their hands on more wealth so that others could respect them. Also so they can have more power over people without money. That's usually done by conquering the territory and the resources from that land to fulfill that saying of money, power and respect. Most people will go to any length to do so; sell their soul if you will.

The old saying goes men should be the provider, which isn't wrong, but it's based on times when things were a little different and it was much easier said than done. Back in the day when the majority of the men were the sole providers, they didn't even have to have degrees. A high school diploma was sufficient to get a job that could take care of the whole family. A lot of men could easily get a job at a factory or something with similar pay and be there for forty years or more right out of high school, and the prices of things was much more affordable so that played a factor also. That's obviously not the case now.

That's another reason having two parent households where both parents contribute are much more relevant now too. It relieves some of the pressure of all the financial responsibility falling on one person. When young males get that embedded into their head and try to live up to that by doing what they have to whether legal or illegal to live up to that saying and sometimes fall victim; victim to not having the proper background or knowledge to get into a business venture or something lucrative. You have to think about the cause and effect of that saying. Being the sole provider means you need enough money to support you and your family with all the household expenses or at least the majority. So males are constantly looking for the quickest route to the money just to keep up with that saying.

Don't get me wrong I think men should be able to provide if they go about things the right way, but they shouldn't have to feel the pressure of trying to be the sole provider. The reason they choose an illegal venture because the money comes quicker than the average working man and they don't have to worry about living from check to check. I understood the philosophy back then but like most of these old written rules and laws they need to be updated with evolving times.

Men should have the financial know-how to make their dollar work for them. Learn how to invest in things that appreciates in value, so it is worth more later on and your dollar grows from the initial investment. Then you're able to sell it for a bigger profit, invest in something larger scale or just dissolve it with profit gains and move on to something else if times get hard but it makes business sense either way. It reminds me off a movie quote I know, "you better make that money, don't let it make you" and what that is essentially saying is don't let the amount of money you make determine what kind of person you're going to be or your personality.

You should always be looking for the financial gain to get ahead of the game of life. You should never want yourself in the position of being one paycheck away from bankruptcy or financial hardship. Start looking at the same business ventures rich folks do to get to that place in life like investments in stocks, bonds, real-estate, collectibles, etc.

Why shouldn't the middle class and lower-class people ever have a chance to make it to the class that most of us want to be at anyway, the upper class? The only thing that keeps the middle and lower-class around is the lack of knowledge. There is so much knowledge out here to enable us to travel similar paths as the upper class but a lot of us never try to gain that knowledge. It's probably because we're not seeking it or seeing it on a frequent basis so it's unfamiliar territory to us and not many people like to charter unfamiliar territory. If the bottom two classes were able to gain the knowledge to keep them from being on the bottom of the totem pole that would possibly eliminate at least one or both of the classes and we could be more alike again.

If you look back at the history of man, it seems like class is another one of those man-made things to separate us from our natural condition or from each other. It used to be based on the different species so that it could be a distinction or separation among them but that was flipped around and turned into something else when currency became a focal point. They used class to not only separate the different species but to make a distinction among a specific species and separate from each other. Mammalia, a synonym for mammal, was the only class distinction as far as humans go and that was based on the species, not having anything to do with the current meaning.

Class is what we are not who we are. As man started to evolve, we start separating ourselves from not just nature but from each other by the amount of money or possessions we had. The whole time, people were slowly forgetting that we are all in the same class. But doesn't that even sound silly? I am classier than you because I have more money than you. It should be based on how you carry yourself with money because I have seen some classless distasteful people in the so-called upper class and all classes.

There are a lot of different ways people can financially reach that class and it's not always in a classy manner. People tend to forget that we are all warm-blooded humans and no one is really different if you take the material things away but who thinks like that anymore?

To me people just wanted to feel superior to others so they could have that male dominating ego fulfilled and in my opinion that ruined society, as we know it. Take that man-made definition away and maybe, just maybe, we could start improving the world like Barack Obama speaks about. Coming together and unifying with one another for one common goal. Everybody should be on the same playing field and have the same opportunities to achieve the American dream of success if you live in America.

Men should know how to be responsible when it comes to their bills. Not outspending more money than they have coming in. Technically you don't have a certain amount of money until you double it and the original amount is put up for savings. You should attempt keep your credit on the positive side of things. There's no reason the bills you acquire should be more than your monthly income. You should have a budget based off your average monthly income no matter if it varies sometimes. If you base it on the highest amount you bring in, it heightens the risk of over spending so you should average it out between the lowest and highest amount. If you spend within your means, then all your bills should be paid on time. That's one way to keep your credit in the positive. Plus it shows that you have a level of responsibility that an adult and a potential leader of a household should have.

You should establish yourself first before you go out and get the luxurious items. If you look at certain people who are trying to achieve wealth, they will walk around in second-hand clothing, drive a used car and remain very basic until their bank account lines up with the type of lifestyle they want to live, or until their revenue reaches a certain consistent plateau. Is the reasoning behind buying expensive items to show you have money? If it is why is it that so many people are losing those expensive items to bankruptcy, repossessions and foreclosures? That is the difference between being rich and being wealthy. The rich have achieved the money to be able to purchase those expensive items but they're either going to be broke after they do it or they can only maintain that type of lifestyle for so long before they go broke. The wealthy usually invest in the smart business ventures or stocks and bonds that create a consistent, flowing, increasing income outside of what they're doing as a career. They wait until they plant their roots in the financial market before they overspend what they don't have. It all adds up pretty quickly and if you don't calculate what that type of lifestyle is going to cost you long-term then the money is here today and gone tomorrow.

It's not always about the material possessions of clothes, cars, houses, etc., but what you have established for you and your kids in the future. That comes by saving and not just spending. How much or how often do you put aside money that you take in, probably not enough. Think about how many parents make their kids save some of the little money they get. When they do get a little money the first thing the parent says is, "you have some money why don't you spend your own." Instead why not tell them to save half of it and spend what you have left over. I bet your child is still going to be happy with being able to spend some of their money on things they want.

You have to train a young mind and develop it with the proper tools needed to be the best them they can be and prepare them for the future. Sometimes it seems that parents forget it's the little things that are vital to the upbringing of the child. This is something I had planned to do with my own kids before they even arrived in the world: have them save at least a quarter to fifty cents of every dollar. It shows them how to spend the money they have while still being able to save some.

Another philosophy I like to refer to help you and your family save is tithing. Tithing is giving ten percent of your earnings through church as a religious ritual to show God that you are willing to sacrifice a financial offering for blessings later. So I say if you can do that for God through a church, why can't you use that same philosophy for yourself if you have a Christ-like mind. Save a percentage of your earnings for yourself religiously, meaning just as often or ritualistically. Why should you rob yourself of savings that you can use for future planning? Think about how much easier it would be to save for a rainy day, save for college, save for retirement, save for an investment and just to save for your future wealth. Do you know how that helps if a child has that type of saving concept instilled early on? The potential that child possesses to have a bright future and be prosperous opens up tremendously.

It doesn't matter if you've become rich or have achieved wealth if you're not right within yourself. It will do more harm than good to have money because you won't know how to handle the pressure that comes with it. There are certain expectations of others for you to be the person to rely on to help them out financially and you might feel pressured to either do so or not. People have a way to make you feel guilty if you don't which could weigh heavy on you.

Trust is something is something you need prior to having money. You need to know who you can trust with your money or around your money so you're not being snaked out of it. You need to know what people's motives are for you or just period, so you know how sincere people are. You have to know who has your best interest at heart. I guarantee you start to see a lot of fakeness if you come into some money, but you need to be able to discern the real from the fake.

A lot of people think just because you get the money the problems will go away, but that's so not true. The more money you have, the more problems begin. It only takes care of the financial problems, but it doesn't remove the pain and the hurt you might feel from old internal scars of family history or just period. I have a great example about having money but not being right internally. I watched an episode from ESPN's *30 for 30* series about a former N.F.L. running back by the name of Ricky Williams. He was in the league for five years and just retired out of nowhere then came back 2 years later. He was one of the young top-tier running backs coming out of college at that time, that received a big money contract potentially worth $68 million dollars but just stopped playing after a few years and nobody really knew why. He later was diagnosed with social anxiety disorder, avoidance disorder, and borderline personality disorder. It probably had a lot to do with him battling old internal scars about being molested by his father.

He kept silent about it until he finally came forward with it as a young boy, which made him feel responsible for the tear in the family.

This was a person who had multi millions and could've moved on from this, but he wasn't healed from this past scar. After his initial departure from the league he ended up practicing yoga and studying medicine to help him deal with what he was feeling internally. He ended up returning to the league eventually and becoming a decent running back again. And by the age of thirty-two he was back to being the running back he once was, which is unheard of. He never gave up, but it wasn't until he dealt with his internal demons that he was able to get back to the top of his game.

So with all that being said deal with your internal self before you even try to dress up the external because if you do it the opposite way it can do more harm than good. That's the reason you see millionaires crumble and become drug addicts, broke, have mental breakdowns, or kill themselves because they're still battling internal demons within. You deal with it by talking about, expressing how you feel about and not holding it in forever as if it never happened.

Credit is another topic that a lot of males don't get an under-standing of growing up. We're never taught what a score is, how to maintain it, how it saves you money and how it affects your life. Males should know if you establish credit and pay your bills on time it will increase your score until it reaches a near perfect score. It's not just about paying bills on time either but learning that the creditors want you to have several open lines of revolving credit with a good repay-ment history of at least a couple years. Also being able to keep your credit spending amount at approximately 30% of your total open line of credit. For example, if you have a $2500 credit limit on the credit cards you have try to keep what you spend at about $750 or lower by the end of each month when the creditors report to the bureaus. It helps raise your score quicker so learn the rules of credit for your own good.

Don't be afraid to get a good financial advisor if you're not good with money. They will help you make wise money decisions and place your money in the right spots so you can see where your money is going. Then you can walk into any place of business and get approved to purchase anything you want on credit if it's within your means and not have to pay a high interest rate on it. That's actually saves you money in the long run. Plus, it gives you a better chance to walk into a bank and get a loan if you are possibly thinking about starting a business, purchasing a home or any big purchases like that where you usually don't have the cash to do so. Now let's be clear, I'm not saying building your credit is an easy thing to do but you have to be disciplined because it's the way of the world.

I know credit doesn't mean a lot to guys who like to purchase things with cash but when you look at it, if you have the cash and still be able to purchase it on credit then you save the money that's in your pocket while having more time to pay it off and build your credit at the same time. That sounds like a win-win combination to me. In addition, you allow more money to come in before you spend a bulk of your money at one time and lessen your chance to overspend.

Hey guys, let me let you in on a little secret; a good woman, not a bad girl, is going to look for a man who is responsible and has good credit once they learn that element of a good man. Another thing about credit that slips through the cracks is how hard it is to get to a near perfect score but how easy it is to go down. That's part of a bigger plan to charge people more money for things unnecessarily but that's a whole other topic. Anyway, learn how the credit works, the rules and the laws of credit and what affects it negatively and positively.

Normally if we're not taught about it, it's probably because our parents weren't that good at maintaining it on their own. They weren't taught themselves or didn't find it important enough to learn how the rules worked. And parents if you weren't good at it and messed up your own credit why use your child's name to mess up their credit instead of repairing yours and showing them what not to do. Now their credit is bad before they have a chance to establish their own because of your negligence. The negative effect of it being bad is it's costing you more money as far as interest rates go and you're not able to purchase things without having a down payment. Plus you always have to depend on somebody for co-signing purposes and most people are hesitant to do that for a person for sake of ruining their own credit for you especially if have damaged your own already.

Sometimes we're not taught things as parents and we have to learn it on the fly, which makes it so much harder. If you know that and had to learn from trial and error, take the time to teach from that space. Show them as a child what you learned as an adult. It's ok to say I didn't know this at your age but I'm equipping you with it now. Don't make your child learn the same way you did.

CHAPTER THREE

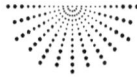

THE DEFINITION OF A LEADER

LEADERS ARE the ones leading the females and children to a much better place in life. They are making sure everyone around them are In the best possible position to succeed. They are covering them under their umbrella of protection through this ugly world and guiding them through the darkness to see a brighter future. They are impacting all their surroundings and affecting change. They are giving you something to look up to.

In all actuality you can make the terms "man" and "leader" interchangeable with each other and every man should want to be the leader of something. Even though we all can't be the leader of the same thing, be a leader at something. There is one thing we all can be a leader of and it's our household and/or family. Who is the first person the child looks up to as a hero or depends on? The parents. And whom does the wife look to for support and advice? Her husband and partner.

Men are the ones who should be helping the woman and child to do better, be better, have better, and live better and in turn it makes the guy better but obviously it's not happening the way it should be. Why do you think so many women are lost in their way of life and so many children are lost without guidance? It's because so many men are falling short. They're forgetting their importance as men and how to be that shining light. It seems to be having an effect on how important and valuable the women feel they are to society.

Women need to find a male counterpart that possesses the proper qualities to be a potential father and leader of the household. To me there should be in-depth conversations about values, parenting, background and future plans with a person of interest before anything sexual takes place so you can know what kind of guy you're dealing with just in case you're faced with life altering event.

Sometimes women have to lower their standards because of the lack of good men they have to choose from. Most of the good men are already taken or just not available to all available women. That's probably why you see a lot more people cheating after marriage. People are tying the knot before they actually get to know whom a person is inside and out and the ratio of good men to good women are so far off. Males know most women are looking for a good man but instead of allowing them to find their own mate or showing them what to look for, they choose to be that good man for them also. Or at least display the qualities but in a wrong situation. And if women just allow it males will take advantage of it time and time again.

A woman once told me while I was engaged that she loves to see when a man shows a commitment by getting married. What maybe was going through her head is even though he's not making a commitment to me at least he's willing to or not afraid to be the type of man a woman needs. Because so many men are unwilling to commit the woman figures I can't get that from my own mate, so I'm intrigued by his willingness. Sometimes women just want to find out what a good man is, what to look for and what they're doing wrong to repel the good ones.

It's so much harder to pass on the proper morals and values if you're not displaying them yourself. Without the proper morals and values the children aren't getting what they need to be successful and productive. It actually increases their chances to be counterproductive and unsuccessful and virtually ends or limits their life before it even starts rolling. If that's the case then there's no hope for the youth, which means there's no hope for the future and that's a lose-lose battle, which will essentially lose the war. No matter what I talk about in this selection it all points back to the man whose actions have the trickle-down effect to the women and children. And until it lines up properly, we're headed down a path of destruction.

Look at it like this: men are like the engine to the car (world) that supply the power and is the main component for the car to work right. But if there's anything wrong that engine and it doesn't get repaired in a sufficient timeframe it might ride rough and not make it to where it's trying to go. So it needs to be in tiptop shape to get the best performance and the smoothest ride it has to offer. Men you should be on top of your game and be the best man you can be for the women you involve yourself with and be the best father for the kids you produce so that their time here on earth is as pleasant, smooth and prosperous as it can be.

Women you are like the tires on the car (world) that keeps the car rolling once it gets moving but you can only ride them for so long before they wear down and potentially pop. Meaning they're there to help the world move forward towards the destination but you can't just put all the pressure on the woman's back to perform alone. Most women can only take so much mentally when taking on a huge load like life by herself without giving in to the pressure and it is causing some sort of breakdown to her mental state. Plus, it's not designed for her too. Instead of replacing the woman like a set of tires you could just keep her feeling fresh and brand new and not make her feel like she has to do it on her own so that she's ok for the long ride of life.

Just remember you can't go anywhere without those tires. They're just as important as the engine is to car. If you're missing any of the tires the car is just a hunk of metal and will not function right until you get some on that car. And the kids are people behind the steering wheel driving to make sure the engine and tires are headed in the right direction to reach the proper destination which is an ideal or happy place in life. The kids should want to give you the drive to work as hard as needed to make life better. If you kids are important to you, you're going to do all you can so that they don't have to live a bad life and suffer as a child or an adult and if both parents are doing their part it makes it that much easier.

A leader could be a leader of himself, leader of his domain, leader of a pack, leader of a state or country but you have to be strong mentally in order to do so. You have to be able to take on your own personal issues and everybody else's that you're the leader of and still be able to make a sound and rational decision while not folding under pressure. He has to have his priorities in order. He has to put God first in his life, his wife and family second, and himself last while fitting his fellow man in there. I want to make sure it's in context though because you might have to wait last to eat but you still have to go hunt to get the food and make sure your family eats.

A leader should not only lead but teach and leave a legacy for himself and kids whether you do that through sports, rapping, business man, doctor, saving lives, or whatever plateau you use to position yourself to make a difference in the world and to another person. I don't know about you, but I would love to be in the history books for something positive. (I would rather not be in there for being the next "American Gangster" either. No offense to show or the people on it because I loved the show but that's not the legacy I want to be known for). I know they were just a group of people who were capitalizing on an opportunity presented to them regardless of what it was. In order to lead and to get people to follow you, you have to show you're able to make the proper decisions in your own walk of life while showing you're not only able to talk the talk but walk the walk.

The people you are leading have to believe you and believe in you and the message or vision you paint for them. When it comes to the household you are the one being looked up to as a role model, hero or a leader so that's more reason you should want to have it together. Men not only are you to be the leaders, the fathers, the husbands and the mentors but you have to be the backbone of the country, communities and households. You are the answer to many of the questions that plague the world in America today. Take a look at some of the issues and see how they point back to the male and how men need to recognize how important they are to the existence of mankind.

By the time you finish reading this project we should be able to look in the mirror at ourselves and see whether we can legitimately be calling ourselves men, or do we need to go back to the drawing board and retool? Adding the necessary qualities needed to get not just us out from under the diminishing statistics but our country, our communities and our households also. Once the men understand the concept of why so many others and I try to reach out to them and encourage them to stand-up and be the best man possible is for sake of a lot of people. It's bigger than us as individuals.

It makes me think of the time when I proudly attended The Million Man March. I was in the ninth or tenth grade at the time and took a lot from that trip. I saw that you could get that many men together and not have any problems or altercations. Everybody had a positive mindset and showed unity. I saw first-hand that men could come together for a common goal on a unified front if they see a purpose. I've never seen men treat each other with such dignity and respect as I did on the ride down there, while I was there, and shortly after.

Now I know this is a different day and age but I greatly believe men are still very capable of a 180 degree about face to change the direction their headed in and become leaders once more. I also saw what happened to the mindsets of the men after the fact and how quickly things changed back to the way it was. I think the message was short-lived because there weren't things set in place or at least I wasn't aware of any, once the males left Washington and went back to their homes so they could carry on the message or mentality of that event. There needed to be things in place nationally and on a statewide level to compound that type of event and bring the help and hope to the individual communities. I believe if people brought all those ideas to reach out to men and give them more options to better themselves, you might get a better outcome of men realizing that you care and really want to help them.

That's one thing I learned the more options you have to be successful the better your chances are to become successful and it's much harder to do with limited options. Like I said before I know its hope for people to change its just going to take a ground level approach and face-to-face talks with people who need guidance and solutions. All you have to do is point them in the right direction to get them there. Sometimes you can say all the right things but if you can't give that individual the attention and help needed it's all in vain. Everybody's situation is different so it can go in one ear and out the other. Most of times actions are so much louder than words and people need to know you can get in the trenches with them, so they have more confidence in you.

For the ones who are in the limelight, you're still looked up to by the kids whether you like it or not because of the lack of role models it is right in front of them and they're looking for somebody to be that for them. Now I understand why certain celebrities say I'm not a role model. They feel they shouldn't have to be a role model to somebody else's child. Plus, they might not have it together themselves but unfortunately the kids don't believe in the people that should be their role models. They're not giving them enough to believe in or a reason to dream big. The kids or the younger generation still want to dream big but their reality around them sets in and their dream gets crushed because they feel they'll never reach that dream. So they look to the celebrities as that vision of hope or leaders.

If people handled their households responsibly, then it wouldn't fall on anybody else's shoulder anyway but unfortunately it has come to that. Speaking on successful celebrities, everybody has different turns and crossroads in their lives so don't think you have to do the same thing somebody else did to achieve financial success or celebrity stardom. Always try to create your own lane and make your own category because it will never be too crowded for you to make it. I do feel like the rappers and entertainers should glorify more of the positive and let the negative be just a quick glimpse instead of vice-versa. The kids are thinking the bad outweighs the good on the way to becoming successful which sometimes it does but they are gravitating towards the negative because that's all they see. If they see the negative all the time in their own surroundings, they should be getting more positive images into their psyche to help drown that out if you really care. Remember you're painting a narrative for someone else to see or hear and they're holding on to every word.

As a leader you should want to be a family man and spend more time with your family rather than running the streets. That shouldn't remain a priority after you mature and chose to settle down and have kids. Their time is much more important than anything you're doing out there unless it's something that is improving the quality of life. Men when you take that leadership away from the household and not play that consistent role; you create an imbalance that throws off the thinking of that child. That child grows up with resentment towards somebody or the world wishing their life wasn't so hard and it affects his or her decision-making process and attitude about life.

You're actually giving that child a 50/50 chance to reach his/her maximum potential and why wouldn't you, the parent gives your child the best chance to achieve success in life which interns has a good reflection on you. You should be the one showing that child how to be a man or in the role of a man and not by beating them on or off camera but showing them how to get up when they get beat down by the world not you. Discipline is to show the child when they are in the wrong there are consequences for certain actions. Not just because they are doing things that a child is likely to be doing anyway and you don't like it or you're not happy with yourself. Let it be a just reason then let them know that you still love them, and it was because of their actions that discipline was even necessary.

You have to break things down to the basics for a child so that they understand what's going on or a person who is childlike. Then the child understands that you can't do anything and get away with it. You should be teaching them how to look you in the face when they speak or when being spoken to so they understand there's a respect factor involved with that and making sure they are comprehending what you're saying. How disrespectful is it to be speaking to someone and they're not paying any attention to you or looking in a whole different direction? You know that they are just waiting for you to end your conversation with them because they're really not listening or don't care. Show them that no matter what you do in life or wherever you work at, you should show good work ethic because it always pays off.

When you work hard and show that you're trying to be something and get somewhere in life it is always recognized by others whether you see it or not. People take notice to hard working individuals. Show them how to earn respect, how to give respect and what it is. They need to know how to make sound decisions. Ideal decisions based on prayer, rationalization, and the betterment of everyone involved not emotional ones.

Know right from wrong and how it affects their life in the future. Show them how to defend their self in case of danger and protect others if need be and not just fighting as an act of anger. It's called self-discipline. They also need to have that same self-discipline in all situations as well. Remember I told you people would try to step on others just to achieve financial success so you can't get angry at everything but know how to handle a situation and be able to recognize genuine people from fake people, so you know if you're being stepped on.

You need to be there to teach them the little lessons in life like riding a bike so when that child falls off you can be there to pick them up and let them know it's ok to fall but don't give up trying. You'll never get anywhere in life if you allow a fall to stop you from getting better or getting to your destination. Be there to calm the child down when they get too excited; keep a cool head in situations and not let their emotions take over the rational thought process. When you're there for the small things in life it teaches the child those little lessons that will go a long way because they will remember what daddy told them, if you're on top of it. Those little lessons translate into life lessons because you can use them when you're older and faced with certain situations. Just make sure you're taking every opportunity to teach and reiterating throughout childhood so they hear your voice when they're at those crossroads in life.

Why can't you be just as effective as the mother is since you are the other 50% of that child's success? Now some areas are going to rely more on the mother's end, and some are going to rely more on the father but at the end of the day it still equals out to a 100% of the child's success. I can't stress enough that's why you have to play your role as a father or leader. You also have to continue to do that after separation regardless of the situation even if the mother makes it a lot harder than it has to be. You have to think about that women gene that thinks with emotion and might be doing that out of hurt or anger not rationalization so it will likely pass. Guys hear that they should marry the mother of their child all the time and I do believe that but to an extent. I think if you go about it the right way initially so that the mother of your child is already your wife or fiancé then you don't have to worry about that. People tend to forget that part when their telling these males that.

Everybody remembers the old saying, "...first comes love then comes marriage then comes baby in a baby carriage." The babies are coming before the love or the marriage and people are trying to correct it with abortions, bad marriages and relationships in order to feel better about going about life wrong. But males you can't compound it by not being there once the children arrive. As a man you have to step up to the plate of responsibility and try to correct it by being there and teaching the child what not to do and not letting them be lost in life like you might have been. When you do things in the proper order of operation, it makes things so much smoother.

To be a leader shows that you're able to stand on your own two feet and make your decisions based on your own thought process and not be easily influenced by others unless it's a positive influence. Learn to trust yourself if you're using the right order of operation in your thought process to come up with answers. Having your own mind and never being a follower of others but doing what you feel is right or best for you without worrying how it makes you look. You have a lot of situations when you're involved in a group and you're doing what the group is doing based on somebody's else's influence but you're not thinking of the impact it has on you as an individual.

To be a leader means you have to be strong mentally as well as physically, so you are able to bare the weight or burden of the world on your shoulders and not collapse under pressure. Remember pressure can bust pipes or make diamonds. When you see people kill them-selves or just give up on life and not the mentally impaired either, they do not have the mental capacity to handle the weight that's being placed on their shoulders and become overwhelmed by the stress of it all. They feel like they have no other route but to end it all or give up and just stop trying.

That's like if you put a person into an enclosed room with no way out and it starts shrinking, a person is going to feel like how I get out of this mess. Especially if this is going to kill me slowly anyway why not put myself out of my misery and do it quickly so I don't suffer? Plus, your mind comes along with so much of its own baggage anyway especially when you have lived a life of turmoil. When you add those extra adult problems it just feels like a ton sometimes. That's why it's imperative that you have yourself together mentally before you decide to add things to the equation of life because unfortunately the world can be very cruel. Don't leave from under your parent's wing unless you have to. At least until you are sure you're ready to fly by yourself. Parents have to do a better job preparing them also before they decide to push them out the nest.

One thing that still confuses me is when people achieve financial success and go and buy the most expensive things they can while people are still living in the streets.

Whatever happened to caring about your fellow man? This just me and my thinking, but why if a person has a million-dollar home can't they downgrade to quarter-million-dollar home and help put a person with no home in a cheap house or any type of housing for that matter. Or if a person has a million-dollar home and only occupied by a few people which is probably more than they actually need and giving a homeless person without addictions a job cleaning up something and/or a place to rest their head. I understand you can't trust any and everybody to invite into your home but sometimes people just need you to believe in them in order for them to turn it around or give them a chance.

This is a philosophy I always use. I give a person one chance to mess over me when I'm presenting them with an opportunity to get ahead and if they mess that up then that's on them. But allow people who are less fortunate a chance before you write them off. Some people don't need handouts sometimes they just need a hand which people seem to stop extending. Instead of just turning your back to everything sometimes it might take just a quick conversation and a small thing to help someone out of their slump. If everybody did at least one thing to make a difference in a positive way in the world we live in it would probably be different than it is now.

The world is crumbling right before our eyes because not enough people thought about more than just themselves and money. And that mentality is going to end the world quicker than we think but maybe that's our destiny for man to destroy themselves.

Maybe that's why you see the satire in movies like "I Robot" and "Eagle Eye" when the machines have to take over and save us from ourselves because who going to protect us from us. I believe we all have more in us than just the ability to work but to make a difference in the world. It's really not that hard to influence one person to dig deeper than the surface and come up with greatness but it just takes work, belief and vision.

CHAPTER FOUR

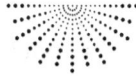

THE IMPORTANCE OF A LEADER IN A HOUSEHOLD

IT ALL STARTS with why it is so important to have that pillar in the home. He creates the foundation to build around. The father provides stability; financially, and materially. He should be setting the tone in the home from the rules, to the environment as a whole. It should be his vision that allows everyone else to know what role they will play in that vision.

If he's removed from his family, it starts a possible trickle-down effect of negativity like single parent homes, money struggles, and a mother trying to be the mother and father. Since she didn't bring the child into the world on her own, she shouldn't have to try to raise the child on her own. That's why it's called parents instead of parent because it takes two to make them and two to raise them. A single parent has to work harder which results in valuable time lost for that child and allows time for that child to be raised or influenced by people other than yourself who may or may not be a good influence. That's when you see the child running with the wrong crowd, allowing his grades to slip, and being raised by people in the streets while making bad decisions along the way.

A male child may feel that he needs to help the struggling parent by doing things to get money legally or illegally and might drop out of school to do so. And if it's illegally, then the crime rates may go up. And if the children don't have the right morals and values instilled, they might try things that put money in the household quickly but without understanding the severity of their decisions. If a young man gets caught doing something illegal, then the prison rates go up and that usually keeps the role models from becoming what they should be for the family because they're not around to do so. Then it leads down a bad path for the future.

How does a child gain understanding of his father not being around for him and his mother? He doesn't. He probably feels like his father doesn't love him and feels abandoned. You can try to replace a missing parent but it's more likely to backfire because most people don't adapt well to new situations or the right person isn't brought into the relationship. The child is already going to have a little resentment or anger towards the missing parent so it might be displayed to the person trying to replace them.

Therefore, the child's respect level is already low because they feel someone is trying to replace the parent, they want to be there in the first place especially if they're not the kind of person who shows they care, demands respect or shows respect towards others. That's why you hear "you're not my father or mother" so much because it's their way of saying you can't replace my parent that I love dearly with a person I barely know. But what can't happen is that the adult lashes back at the child because they feel disrespected.

It's probably a natural reaction, but as the adult you have to realize the situation and approach it properly. You'll never get through that way. What that person who's coming into the picture has to do is say to that child that "I'm not trying to be them or replace them, but I do want to be here for you and show you love too". It would help take down the wall that the child has up and build up a comfort and respect level so there can be understanding.

Not many kids know how to express their feelings and emotions, so they display it through acts of anger or other attention getting acts. Plus, kids emulate what they see so if they see marriage, hard work, love and respect in their household then they're going to emulate that as an adult. But if they see the parent with different people, selling drugs, disrespectful, lazy, etc. they're going to emulate that, so watch what you put into your child's spirit. But if you're not married, that could start tension between the mother and the father about the whole marriage issue and result in a person leaving the situation if they're not ready for marriage so be weary of that.

So guys, before you step away and decide not to be a part of your child's life on an everyday basis, think about how much you didn't like for your father not to be there. How much pain and confusion it caused in your life, then look in your child's eyes and realize you're going to be doing the same to them. Don't be afraid to fight for something. Your child is worth the fight. It's a fight to save the God given structure of family. If you know anything about psychology you also know that most people have a fight or flight mentality. It usually happens when tension is high, fear sets in or a person just doesn't know what to do. Most people take flight or retreat as a defense mechanism, but few are willing to stand in the face of adversity for a better tomorrow.

Which one are you?

CHAPTER FIVE

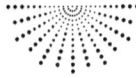

THE DEFINITION OF R-E-S-P-E-C-T

RESPECT IS something that is earned, not given. In order to get the respect you deserve, you have to be willing to give it to others. Treat people how you want to be treated. You also have to respect yourself. Don't allow people to disrespect you because they will if you let them. They shouldn't be able to talk to you a certain way, mistreat you, do you any kind of way that's not loving and belittling you. People won't give you the respect if you don't respect yourself.

When you walk outside your private doors you should handle yourself in a respectable manner; respecting yourself and others. Respect is one of those words I think is lacking in the newer generation and that has an effect on the older generation too. The reason I say that is because the older generations were taught about respect, so they understand the concept and meaning behind it. Since the younger generation lacks that knowledge and concept, they don't give the respect like they should so they don't receive it like they should from the elders. In order to earn respect, you have to give it. It's never just given. Plus, you need to handle yourself in a mature manner and then you can get that respect that men so eagerly yearn for.

When you're in public you should watch the cursing, the smoking, the drinking, the loud music, and any other inappropriate actions that would cause you to look foolish. There's a reason I say, "watch it" instead of just plain "don't do it!" For one, you shouldn't tell anybody what to do or not to do if you're not a relative or somebody who has earned the respect from that person because we all know most people don't like being told what to do. That's why you see incidents of people cursing people out if you try to suggest what somebody shouldn't be doing.

Second, even if you do that kind of stuff it can still be done with discretion. There's a time and a place for everything. For instance, if you're around a crowd of people who do some or all of the same things you do then it's more appropriate, maybe not right but more appropriate. Rather than if you're in a residential neighborhood or around a family with kids, parents or grandparents, and you don't see any of the same actions taking place then it makes it less appropriate.

If respect was one of those things you were taught, you wouldn't do certain things that would disrespect others anyway. I'm not saying this because I'm one of those people who feel you need to be a certain way in the public eye because you're still a human being, but I do feel you should respect yourself and the way you're viewed by others. It's called self-respect. To me, people in the public eye shouldn't be put on a pedestal or held to a higher standard anyway but viewed as inspiration to what you can become even with your flaws and hard work.

Since we're talking about respect, let's not forget the respect of the ladies or the lack thereof. For a long time, I couldn't understand why so many males treated women so poorly and why women took it. One thing I do know is if the women decided not to take the disrespect and demand more from the guys, the men would have no choice but to step it up and fall in line. Whether they admit it or not, men need women more than some let on. Most men won't turn to another man the way women can turn to each other for comfort, compassion, and companionship so they have no choice but to rely on the women for it. They're too macho for that.

We all know men would do whatever it takes to get close to a woman whether it's for companionship, sexual purposes, or to establish a family. So it's up to the women on how they're treated by men because they hold more power than they think. If respecting a woman is beneath you to do, then you completely have it wrong. Tupac Shakur stated it very well when he said, "We all came from a woman, got our name from a woman, got our game from a woman. I wonder why we take from our women, why we rape our women, do we hate our women.

It's time that we kill for our women, time to heal our women, be real to our women and if we don't, we'll have a race of babies that will hate the ladies that make the babies." If the father was disrespectful towards the mother when he got with her and the mother accepted the disrespect to end up with him, what are the chances of the child to have a disrespectful upbringing and lack respect?

The disrespect of yourself and others goes back to how you were treated as a child. I talk about respecting yourself and others who live in the same household as you in an upcoming section of the book about private life. And that's where the finger points if you want to pinpoint the problem. When kids are taught and shown respect, they grow up using that same value toward others but when they are taught and shown the opposite, they do the opposite. How can a child know anything different other than what they see every day? Even if someone tries to show them differently it has to be more than just temporary, because it won't overcome the years of things being instilled in that child and would likely get drowned out. There has to be a complete change of positive scenery for an extended period of time in order to completely change the mentality of that child who has seen otherwise their whole life. Some things you can't explain to a child because they're too young to understand the concept, but if you show them, they'll pick it up visually before they would verbally.

If we were able to observe every household and track back like a family tree, you would be able to find the problems that occur with kids and their behavior. Somewhere down the line a kid didn't get the proper or needed attention from one or both parents and started doing something out of line. If behavior never got addressed, then the child continued the inappropriate behavior or got worse and it sometimes breeds more wrong behavior and thoughts psychologically. So it possibly passes down and has a cause and effect on the next generation. You probably could pinpoint each generation's issues within the family spectrum that put them on the path they are on. You can wish to reach back to change everything and put it all on the right path but you can't.

You can't be around kids and doing things that are disrespectful to them like excessive drinking, smoking, cursing, sexual acts, etc. What that does to the child is give them the impression that it is a normal thing to do and it spills over to the public side all because you didn't respect them privately. Even if you try to verbally explain the wrongs and make them seem ok for you the child is going to grow using the same philosophies and always make their wrongs right for themselves. So in their eyes, it's never disrespectful to do certain wrongs whether it be public or privately because not only were they not taught, but because they weren't shown. They need to be taught and shown how to talk the talk and walk the walk.

So what needs to be done is people need to repair the problems within their own household currently by establishing the basic fundamentals of life like morals, values, respect, responsibility, family, and love so that it's translated into everyday life and kids won't misrepresent themselves and/or the parent/guardian. Kids can't raise themselves so the right things need to be instilled in them from birth and throughout their life so their principles are solid. Kids can't raise kids either so try to avoid being a child having a child because you still have much growing and learning to do yourself before teaching another.

I have an experience or example I'd like to share with you about private matters spilling over to the public due to lack of respect. I was at a gathering at a family member's house where it was the family that lived there then other friends and family over that didn't live there. During the outing, two of the family members that were from the household proceeded to have a heated altercation. It was between a step-mother and a step-son and it started off subtle with a few back and forth forms of sarcasm but got a little more disrespectful and ended with a you're not my mother quote that I mentioned earlier. It was surprising to everyone because it happened so suddenly and never gotten to that before but in all actually it was probably building up prior to that night.

I'm sure it had something to do with the difference in personalities between his actual mother that had passed which probably still harbored pain in his heart and the step-mom. He probably felt a little disrespected by the way he was being handled or talked to by the step-mom that night or maybe in general because I don't think it would've exploded from one incident if it weren't a buildup of emotion. In my opinion, that situation could've been handled much differently so that it wouldn't have ruined a fun night or been an embarrassment. The step-son could've pulled the step-mother to the side at that particular time and addressed what he felt was disrespect, or he could've waited until everyone was no longer present to do so and not go off in the middle of an audience out of respect.

Another scenario is the stepmother should've shown more respect towards the young male and chose her words more wisely since there was an audience and he would've felt less disrespected. Like I said, there is a time and place for everything.

That's what happens when you don't respect whom you live with and not keeping private matters private, so they don't spill over. Once it reaches the public there is a defense mechanism that kicks in, so you don't feel belittled especially when it comes to males because of the male macho trait we have. I'd like to call it an instinct because that's what it should be. You should be able to turn the mechanism on and off like an animal instinct and not just react. Women also have that same kind of cat-like instinct when it comes to being belittled in front of an audience.

When it comes to people you work with, hang with or sleep with there's always a possibility for things to get out of hand, but it's all about how it's handled. When you have that respect factor it keeps any situation from getting out of hand and resulting in an unwarranted altercation. When a male's manhood is tested, he feels he has to do whatever it takes to get it back or maintain it especially when it comes to the people he's sleeping with and emotions that could be involved.

Emotions are one of those things that a lot of men haven't learned how to deal with or handle properly. It will quickly escalate any situation when you care about someone or put pride first. We will get into that a little later. People tend not to understand or downplay the situation of sleeping with someone and the severity of it. It comes with a lot of ramifications.

A woman is choosing to give you a piece of her soul and heart, and if you violate it by putting personal business out to the public or continuously do things to take pieces of her soul and heart, you're doing more damage than you think. First of all, guys you can get a woman to do whatever you want if you treat her right and have her back. So calling yourself a pimp or player because you tell all these lies to manipulate her to get her to do something that's already in a woman's nature to nurture and take care of is really neither a pimp nor a player. It's really considered taking advantage of someone which is wrong morally.

CHAPTER SIX

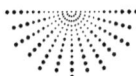

D EFINE YOURSELF FROM THE INSIDE OUT

THIS IS the time where we learn what we are made up of internally and how we deal with the mental component. We have to find out what traits we should possess and what we may lack so we know what adjustments we need to make to become a complete man. We have to solidify our mental toughness and fortitude in order to be able to handle what it takes to be at the forefront of it all.

Now it's time to get into the mental aspect of a man where it gets long and complicated but let's dive right into it. This is where a lot of men are going to accept or reject the ideas of manhood, but this is going to make you a better man if you soak it up and apply it and not be too macho to listen to good useful advice. "The way of a fool seems to be right to him, but a wise man listens to advice." (Proverbs 12:15). Wise intelligent people are going to listen or hear good things that will make them better as people, but foolish people will reject it. God created man to be a provider, teacher, protector, cultivator, visionary, leader, and to reproduce.

God gave man work in the Garden of Eden and that was strategic so that man could provide for himself and for the others he would be responsible for. There had to be somebody who could hunt or gather food for the woman and the others that he was responsible for when they weren't capable of, and to insure the garden was taken care of so it could continue to produce crops.

There also had to be a leader to show them the necessary survival skills in order to survive on their own and be the example of how a leader should operate as the head of the family, and also how to be a protector of himself and all that belongs to him. There had to be someone around to protect the family and the assets from imminent danger because there has always been some type of danger lurking in the mist. Who best to protect them than the more physically dominating male who is capable of defending what's his?

The young male must be shown how to protect himself if he's faced with life threatening or harmful circumstances while still showing constraint and self-discipline. This is where he needs to be in control of his anger or emotions, so he doesn't quickly jump off the deep end and cause harm to another person and face life-changing circumstances unless he is forced to, not just because he's insulted with words or something minor. Because as you mature as a man, you're likely to look back at it and realize the minor things weren't even worth the life change.

"A fool shows his annoyance at once, but a prudent man overlooks an insult." (Proverbs 12:16). This is just pretty much saying a man should be able to keep a cool head for minute things. I believe the reason they use the word fool so much is to have a reverse effect on the person reading it. Most people feel they are not fools or foolish, but if you are acting in a foolish manner then you need to adjust your actions so that it doesn't insult you similar to the way it did me when I read it. That's why it's good to take up things like martial arts because it teaches you rules like patience and self-discipline.

God also wanted us to be a cultivator which means to make something better than when you first receive it. Pretty much anything you come in contact with and can affect change onto it especially the woman. Single guys should be making the women that they deal with in their lifetime better than they were before they start dealing with them. Don't be afraid to lead and teach the women that need it if you're capable of doing so because sometimes women want us to be similar to a father figure. Take them by the hand and show them the way to a better life. Don't be afraid to learn and try to understand them too.

Now I'm not saying that's an easy task but it is very possible to learn their strengths and weaknesses so you can help improve the weaknesses and build off their strengths, the same way you would do a daughter or a son. That's probably why you hear women call their men daddy sometimes.

Married men, if you have envisioned how you want your wife to be, you have to make sure you equip her with the right tools and information needed to be the best wife for you and if you don't do that you can't blame her for not knowing. Now if you tell her time and time again and she doesn't take to the information given then that's a different story.

Men, we have to have a vision about our life and where want it to go. We have to envision ourselves in the position of influence that's positive and are willing to go after that vision with a plan that's realistic, step by step and maintain your focus all the way. What's the point of having a dream if you can't make it come true? A lot of us males lack vision and wonder why we don't become leaders and end up followers of others' visions. If you have a significant other and you wonder why she won't follow you through the fire or submit to you, it may be because you haven't painted the right picture for her to believe in. She needs that if she's going to trust your word and follow it.

As for the women who follow men with no vision you're destined to bump into the same obstacles or walls as him because the blind can't lead the blind. If you see where it's headed but wants to hold on for the ride just for the sake of a male figure around, then shame on you. If you don't jump off the ship before it crashes, then you're going to get burned from the fire time and time again.

Last, we were put here to be leaders, capable of leading a pack to the necessary place that enables our survival. We must teach the next generation what must be done in order to lead a pack themselves.

Train them up to be future leaders. We have to show them what it takes and the responsibility that comes with being a leader and also how to display the characteristics of one. A leader is also a servant, disciplined, the first one up and the last to sleep. He sets the tone, has integrity, strong, character, and his word is his bond. A man does not carry a grudge; he always looks to be the best him and invests in his success, gives to his community and should be judged by his character.

By nature, man (humans) inherits curiosity, gentleness, intimacy, responsibility, enthusiasm, sensuality, tolerant, courageous, honest, vulnerable, affectionate, proud, spiritual, committed, wild, nurturing, peaceful, helpful, intense, compassionate, happy and able to express emotion.

A person named Aaron Kipnis breaks down man into three stages of masculinity in the book, "Knights without Armor": heroic masculinity, feminized masculinity, and authentic masculinity. The heroic masculinity was likely based on the old male principles during the time of medieval wars, so males needed to be this way. "It's physically hard, dominating, tough, soldier, killer, coercive, controlling, lord and master and destructive. It is emotionally closed, numb, codependent, demanding, and aggressive, cynical, sex partner, defensive and repressed. Mentally it's compartmentalized, penetrating, analytical, splitting, linear, hierarchy, exploitive, rules and laws."

The feminized masculinity is based on the more traditional principles. "It's being physically soft, submissive, gentle, pacifist, gatherer, and pliant, controlled, consort, immobile. Emotionally it's more unprotected, flooded, dependent, smothering, passive, naïve, pleaser, wounded, contained and nice. Mentally is merged, diffused, synthetic, joining, circular, anarchy, conservative, procedures, magical and thinker. Spiritually matriarchal, dualistic, seeker, in fight, selfless, disassociated belief, inclusive and guru."

The final component is the authentic masculinity which is based on the new male principles. "It is physically flexible, capable, strong, warrior, hunter, firm, vigilant, husband/partner, generative. It's emotionally receptive, feeling, and interdependent, nurturing, assertive, fresh/humorous, lover, deep feeling, wild and playful, fierce. And mentally eclectic, insightful, discriminating, holds paradox, holonic, community, resourceful, personal ethics, and healer. And spiritually is polytheistic, paradoxical, initiated, grounded, braided self, embodied, direct experience, selective and mentor/elder."

If you look at the heroic term which used the old principles, it probably comes from the more male dominated era when women were suppressed, and men didn't really cater to women's feelings or take into consideration much. Some men still go by those principles and never allow the woman to blossom and become better. They're still trying to shatter their confidence to make them feel like they can't accomplish things, probably because they're scared the women might become better than them and surpass them in certain areas when their allowed to put forth the same effort. But little do you know the better the woman is the better you'll be because you're going to strive to maintain your male dominance and be just as good or better.

It's not a competition or anything but just making each other better individuals. "Submission was designed by God to yield a synergistic relationship, where the two work together to produce a result greater than the sum of their individual capabilities." Really, I want to focus on the part where it says the two work together because it's really about bouncing off each other's strengths and learning how to work together to make each other stronger to achieve one common goal. I heard Will Smith say in an interview you are who you're around and the five closest people to you should be better than you are and that gives you something to strive for.

So maybe it does turn into a friendly competition but that's a good thing for the both of you. That's just the competitive spirit in us to be the best. To me that keeps you from becoming content which most of us tend to do anyway. If you look at it, when we reach a certain plateau, we get complacent and don't try to take it to the next level. We stop at average and never go for above average or the best which we all should be shooting for anyway; the best you.

If you still go by the heroic or chauvinistic principles it could leave you on the outside looking in when it comes to keeping a modern-day woman happy. You need to possess some of those feminized masculine qualities in order to fulfill some of those most important needs a woman has.

If you look at same-sex dating amongst women, a lot of women decided to go that route after they weren't getting what they needed from men. You see more women relationships now more than ever before, but can you blame the ladies who are tired of not getting the complete package from males that they are dating. The women are stepping up feeling like they can do a better job than the no-good men because they feel they're more capable of meeting the needs of a woman. There's no way women should be trying to take our place as men because not enough of us are stepping up to the plate and fulfilling a woman's needs. And men should not be trying to take the place of women.

Some women are walking around looking and acting more like men than men and some men are walking around looking and acting more like women than women. Doesn't something seem wrong with that picture? The downside to the women immolating men is that a lot of women are immolating the same misconstrued player image that a lot of us have soaked up and having some of the same issues that we have in our relationships with women. The same goes for the men immolating women, they're immolating something based off a perception rather than actually having the instincts of that gender and knowing how to behave as one and it comes off very misconstrued.

Something I notice with either immolation that seems to get overlooked is the lack of commitment that people are willing to make regardless to who they're in a relationship with. It could have something to do with people not really understanding what a commitment is and what it takes to make a serious commitment. One thing about a woman if she doesn't get certain attributes from her last relationship, she'll be swept off her feet by the next person who brings what the last person lacked and now a days it's not just males who are trying. Women are more willing to date who ever says they can give them what they need and be their better half.

But one thing about that same-sex dating is you can't replace what God made for us and that's a man for a woman and a woman for a man and the certain elements made to complete the cycle of life. I'm not going to pretend like I know why we were put here on earth and what's our purpose but one thing I do know is that we are made to be reproducing creatures and that can only be done with what God has put in place for us to maintain life; a man and a woman. Every time I see women together in public, I just shake my head because I pretty much know it was a male's fault in some kind of way, whether directly or indirectly. It could be sexual abuse, mistreatment, lack of leadership or just removing of self all together but the roads usually leads to men directly or indirectly.

That's why people say men need to get in touch with their feminine sides so that they can be more receptive to women's feelings and needs. That doesn't mean you have to become a homosexual or strut around being feminine. It just means learning a woman, studying a woman, understanding a woman so you can know how to react to their actions since theirs is usually based on emotions. Without it you're going to think everything a woman does is insane and not going to want to deal with it because you don't understand what's going on. That's usually what happens when someone doesn't understand something, they just push away from it.

That's why it's so important to have two parents in the home because it doesn't allow the young child to get confused by the upbringing of a one parent system. If there is a mother raising a male and that male stays on the straight and narrow while remaining by his mother's side it's likely that you see that male with a lot of feminized qualities of his mother as he grows up because he didn't have that balance of masculine qualities that a father would've brought to the table. You might hear him being called a "momma's boy" sometimes.

That's why you see boys in elementary, middle, or even high school having their manhood questioned. They grow up trying to prove their manhood by doing things they think men would do like fighting, getting girls, getting money or just showing off period to prove their male dominance. It's usually things they see guys doing around the neighborhood or on T.V. and nobody's questioning their manhood so that's where the misconstrued view comes in at. They figure I must need to be doing that kind of stuff, so no one is questioning me.

If a woman is raising a woman there are too many hormones within one household or too much of the same thought pattern which usually leads to a clash because there's no one there to intercept and rationalize a situation when there becomes one. When a man is raising a male, the young male misses out on the feminized qualities that a mother provides like being thoughtful, compassionate, nurturing, gentle and a little submissive that he needs to become an authentic man.

He normally doesn't do those types of things when it comes to dealing with his child and they need it. He doesn't always need to be told to shut up, man up, get hit or beat down. Sometimes he just wants to cry to get it out and listened to and calmed down. Sometimes he just wants to be shown love and talked to so you can get to the root of the problem and come up with the best possible solution.

That child needs you to be physically soft at times, so he doesn't think he has to build up a hard-shell-like exterior and be hardened to everything and everybody. But he still needs to be able to stand-up in the heat of battle if needed. If it's a male raising a girl, he can't answer some of those questions that only a woman can answer because as a man he just doesn't know, or he might not be sensitive enough to understand what a woman goes through, or he just doesn't feel it's his place as a father.

The raising of a child alone can only work if you have strong family support that can step in and help you in areas that you need it. It doesn't matter if it's a woman or man raising a child alone just remember to bring the best qualities of parenthood you can to the table so that your child gets at least the best of what you have to offer. You can give your child all the material things world but are you willing to give them you.

As for me I understand that aspect of parenthood as far as being the best parent I can even though I'm still trying to get better. I will never stop attempting to elevate. I can take care of my daughters from the time they wake up to the time they go to sleep by myself, from head to toe. It's not because their mother isn't around, but I feel I'm just as good of a parent as she is, so why should she have to do it all herself. I do things for and with my daughters that most guys wouldn't be caught dead doing because I am confident in my manhood and my parenting skills.

Guys don't feel that you can't do your job as a parent if the mother isn't around and you feel something is her job. I can assure you they're not waiting on you to be a father if you're not around and if they are, they're not showing it. They are moving right along and trying to be as much of both parents as possible so I'm sure you're just as capable of being a parent as she is and not just the father. Sometimes you need to step up and play a role that might go against your "manhood" with instincts that are naturally inherited from your mother. But at the end of the day you're still a man and probably a better one because of it.

As men I think we're too worried about what the next so-called man is going to think or say if we are doing certain parenting duties when needed. Do everything you can in your power to give your children the best of you. Don't be afraid of ridicule if it's in the best of interest of you and your child. But if you are confident within yourself then no one can question you or your reasoning behind your actions.

The authentic masculinity to me seems to be the heroic and the feminized masculinity rolled into one. As you can see Aaron Kipnis used the word "authentic," authentic meaning real, and once you get to that certain level you can be labeled a real man. Until then you're just a male searching for what it is to be a man and losing out on valuable time. You have to know how to use those male instincts when needed and the feminized instincts when needed also that all of us males need in us to become authentic.

Like I said earlier, being too heroic can hurt you, but being too feminized could too. Most women aren't going to want a man who's too submissive, dependent, smothering, passive, and naïve; nor are they going to want a man who's too dominating, aggressive, controlling, destructive, emotionally closed, numb, or exploitive either.

You can't be too physically hard and you can't be too physically soft, you definitely have to be physically flexible so you can adapt to different situations especially when it comes to dealing with your woman and child, even with dealing with your fellow man. The qualities man inherits by nature almost coincide with the qualities that an authentic man consists of. So you are naturally born with the proper qualities but are losing them along the way, somehow probably due to children not picking up enough of both parents' traits since there's usually not two around.

I know it sounds like a lot to achieve full authenticity of manhood but don't forget you have a lifetime to reach it, and you only have to take one step at a time. But the sooner you get started, the faster you can become that ideal man. Let's not forget women have a biological clock and are looking for the first person who can provide her with the things she is looking for to build a family with so let's get on the ball. The sooner you start building your brand and legacy, the more people you can have a positive effect on and change the course of history.

Now let's take a little closer look at some of the authentic qualities that men should possess. Women want a strong warrior who's capable to stand-up to just about anything, in or outside the household when faced with obstacles and tough decisions and stands behind his solid decision. A woman needs to know the man is smart and confident so they can be reassured they're not being led in the wrong direction and that he knows what he's doing.

There are probably a few, but how many women do you know that just wants sex partners. Women are potentially looking for a husband and life partner to build a family with, not just a person who they're going to see come and go or who they have to track down once they're not around. They want a special bond with one male who's just a phone call away if they're not around or who they can depend on for any and everything. He needs to be reliable and consistent. If males were raised up to be the best men they could be, I think you would see a lot more marriages because women would have more choices to choose from and a lot less divorces. All they really want to feel is that security that a man should be providing whether it is financial or physical protection and if you lack that what do they have to fall back on.

Women want a man to be more receptive to their emotional needs because we all know women can get overly emotional at times. But it's in their nature and they just want us males to cope, listen, console and calm them down when it gets like that. With all due respect, as I mentioned before, the same way you would do a child. There are certain things a child has to learn before they can apply it. The same can go for an adult who hasn't learned certain things. The reason I stated it like that is because like I mentioned earlier when you learn and understand a person and what they lacked in their childhood then you can build a person up and fuse those qualities in with a very sensitive approach.

Women want us to understand what they're going through at that time so we can help them through that phase because that's all it is a phase. Something that is going to come and go, and you should be able to handle it for the moment. By not getting upset either because you don't want to hear it but with a shoulder to cry on until the tears stop flowing. They just want an ear for them to vent to and listen to them or the calming voice that eases the burden and relaxes them for the moment.

It's called being tolerant; being able to sit through something that normally irritates you. Plus you shouldn't want to see your loved one in turmoil so why not be a willing participant to make it better. One thing women don't understand about us males is that we do a lot of things because we know we have to not because we want to. And that's not necessarily a bad thing, but it is the case so don't hold us at fault if we're not enthused about everything we do. That can always go both ways. We do what we have to at least until we care enough to want to do it on our own.

You should at least act like you care and respond in a certain manner. Say those things certain things that women need to hear at times about their looks, appearance, intelligence. Give her compliments just because. Not to get sexual favors either, but to boost their confidence and self-esteem and to encourage and motivate them to be better, do better, and feel better.

I've had women tell me, "Whether you mean it or not just say what I need to hear because I need that" and that's indicative to the message I'm trying to relay here. Besides they really won't know how sincere you are or not when you say it and sometimes, they don't care but until you build that confidence up to a certain level it just needs to be done often. You should be complimenting them on their physical and mental attributes so they know you feel a certain way about them and are paying attention to them.

Males wonder why women need to hear that all the time, but it probably comes from the lack of compliments the parent(s) gave to that child. People tend to forget that a child should be complimented frequently on how smart and beautiful or handsome they are so by time they're an adult they're already confident enough not to need it as much, or at all because it's already instilled in their psyche. A rapper by the name of Jada kiss said a line that stuck with me, "I'm not cocky I'm confident so when you tell me I'm the best it's a compliment." It's a song lyric, but it's kind of what I'm talking about as far knowing who you are and how you feel about yourself before anybody even opens their mouth to tell you.

Men don't be afraid to be emotional or express emotion when it's needed because it helps relieve you of tension and anger. If you try to be to physically hard and not release the emotion that's building up inside of you that is a natural thing, it can turn that into rage and that's when it becomes a problem. Males aren't good with dealing with emotion because they're usually taught or learn to be so physically hard that it seems unnatural or unmanly when they finally allow it or it's forced out by an event or love it's handled all wrong.

That's why you see a lot of jealous rages and a lot of senseless killings because males haven't learned how to express or release those pinned up emotions without feeling like less of a man. But if you're confident in your manhood, that shouldn't be a problem because you're still going to be a man once those tears dry up or the anger is released.

There are a lot of things going on within a person's mind when love and emotions are involved. Because women deal a lot more with love and emotions during pregnancy and more serious relationships, they're used to feeling vulnerable at times, so they have learned how to deal with it much better than us males who tend to shy away from that as much as possible. We would rather stay away from something serious than deal with the emotional side of it. We don't want to be taken over by emotion because it takes away from rational thought process and we don't like the feel of that. It makes us feel like we're not in control anymore. Sometimes we're just scared to let go and be a certain way because it leaves us feeling vulnerable.

"To willingly become susceptible to another requires a high level of trust in the relationship. Therefore, for you to build a lasting fruitful relationship requires both time and effort. The more you know about someone, the more you feel you can trust that person. The more you can trust, the more vulnerable you allow yourself to be with the person." So there definitely has to be a trust factor there before you allow yourself to be vulnerable and if you don't have that, that means there's still some work that needs to be done or you're dealing with the wrong person.

Allow time to grow and study each other with a willingness to do so. Understand each other's boundaries and thresholds to keep from pushing an unnecessary button. Everybody wants to know they can trust a person with their heart and feelings so it doesn't get stomped on.

A lot of times people allow themselves to be vulnerable, mostly women, before they build up a certain level of comfort and trust. Not with men though. They're going to do everything possible to not allow that vulnerability to show. That could be why a lot of males involve themselves in physical combat whether professional or non-professional because that's a way of release. If we can scream, punch, kick, or shoot it filters out that emotion or anger from the heart and mind and channels it through our mouth, hands or feet. Guys you have to realize women like to see a guy who shows emotion, vulnerability, and tears because it shows them that you're willing to open up and be vulnerable and intern makes them feel more comfortable with you.

Women want to know that you're able to have deep feelings to show them that you're deeper than a puddle of water but well deep. They also want to know that your train of thought is just as deep, so they know you're thinking about more than just what is in front of you and the present time. I guess what I'm trying to say is a grown man should have substance about himself and not be afraid to love and trust but like I said that comes with time and mutual effort. But make sure it's with a person who has the attributes you're looking for to make you happy. It should be about more than just money and sex especially if you want to end up happy. It needs to show that you're thinking ahead and about you're future because it shows the women that she has a chance to be involved in your future plans if she's a viable candidate.

Once you attempt to pursue a partner, you need to stay fresh and humorous to ensure that your partner doesn't get bored with you after a long period of time. To stay fresh means that you're continuously doing or saying new things to your partner that keeps her surprised because it's unexpected. You also have to do new things like finding new places to go on dates and trips to show her that you're constantly thinking of new ways to impress her. She wants you to always flirt with her the same way you would with somebody new and show interest. She always wants to feel like the girl you want, the girl you want to be around, the girl you want to talk to and the girl that you're sexually attracted to. She wants to be your safety net along with you being hers.

But the ladies also have to remember to do new things and stay fresh too, to ensure that they receive that freshness back from their significant others. You can start by keeping your physical person looking a certain way or as physically fit as possible. You want your mate to be looking at the same person he fell in love with not a totally different looking person even though it shouldn't matter but it does. You don't want his perception of you to change.

You also have to make sure you're doing new and sexy things and changing little things with your appearance so there's something a guy can notice and compliment you on. But remember this goes both ways because what can't happen is guys you can't lose your physical appearance that was an attraction for your significant other in the first place too. You at least want to attempt to maintain as best as possible.

They say that laughter is a big key to happiness because it keeps you relaxed and at ease and helps the stress level lower so being humorous is important. I'm not talking about being a goof ball either, because there's a chance that people might not take you seriously. You can't be overly serious all the time either because it will keep you tense and possibly raise your stress level.

Depending on a person's sense of humor because everybody is different, you should at least attempt to keep a smile on her face by whatever type of humor you possess. The best thing to do is get with someone who thinks your sense of humor is funny and laughs at your jokes. I've dealt with people who thought I was hilarious and I've dealt with people who didn't quite get my style of humor, not many of course but it can vary so be weary of that.

A male should be insightful and knowledgeable in many different areas so that when you're asked a question by your partner or anybody for that matter, you are able to come up with an answer or at least know where to get one from; be resourceful. Your woman is going to ask you random questions sometimes because they expect you to know it all even if you don't. She will love to not have to go outside her marriage or relationship for answers or anything for that matter and it is a turn on for women if their man is smart as he is handsome.

I had a woman tell me: I love when my man can give me the answers to my question no matter how far-fetched it is. The more knowledge you receive and maintain the more it allows you to depend on yourself and rely less on others. You know, trust yourself.

Now you're capable to come up with the answers to get the job done. It could also help you save time and/or money in the long run. If you noticed people over charge because they have expertise in a certain area. They know you need them to take care of whatever it is you're paying them for, but if you have that knowledge to come up with answer you might be able to do little things yourself. People probably don't even realize, the more knowledge you have at the time of conception of a child the more you pass on to that child through genetics even though a child is born with their natural learning instincts.

Have you ever noticed if the parent has a special God-given talent or just good at a certain thing that their child is usually blessed with similar talents or abilities? Along with God playing his role, that is done with genes that are genetically passed down to the child through the parents. As a parent, make sure you help them utilize their abilities and never let them fall behind.

A man has to be nurturing towards his significant other and his child to let them know that in their time of pain or discomfort he is there for them. There to make them feel better and let them know it's going to be ok. Sometimes it's not always that bad, but they might just need the attention to let them know there is somebody there to love them in the time of need. There are plenty times my kids might fall and scrape or bump themselves. I just give them a little extra special attention and ask them is it ok now. They stop crying and tell me yeah and go back to whatever it is they were doing so it does work. Bring a calm to the situation.

I also want to take a look at some of the things man (human) inherits by nature. We are a curious species because we need to know what things are. We need to know what's going on around us and how things are working the way they are. That's probably where scientists originated from because of our need to figure these things out. Since we are reproducing creatures, the human side of us is going to be intimate and sensual because that's part of courting and we are developed with feelings. It turns our reproduction process into a different deeper situation.

But now that it has reached that point and we know our mate wants to be touched in a certain fashion or enjoys being intimate and sensual with her mate. We should adapt to that and provide her with a certain feeling of intimacy through sensitive and sensual places especially when there is love involved. Intimate and sensual don't always have to be physical things either. They can include a mental connection too. It can be just thinking the same thing or wanting the same thing.

We are normally gentle creatures by nature. It's not until we are forced to protect ourselves or until we defend our own in battle or become hunters and gatherers for survival that we become aggressive in nature and are forced to harm or kill. It's our animal instinct that brings it out but when we are protecting and in battle, we have to become courageous in order to survive it. We also still have to be gentle with our own mate and kids, so they know they're in good hands. That's part of being a nurturer; the caring loving side of us which is something that should be in both parents because we both have to care for our children. We just bring that different element to the table in raising our children and it gives that even mixture of fulfillment that completes the child.

As a nurturer you're supposed to be gentle and tolerant when necessary. Other times you have to be firm, fierce and honest. Because we have patience and there's a threshold to that, we have to be tolerant of little things in order not to reach that threshold too fast. We become aggressive if that line gets crossed, so we have to be firm and fierce when telling a person not to push certain buttons. No matter who it is, when someone tells you that believe them because you don't know their threshold especially when people are already on edge from life.

We also have to be firm and fierce when it comes to enforcing rules and discipline so who's ever receiving it knows that you're serious. We have to always be honest, well as much as possible even if a person doesn't like it. But at least you give them the choice, or they know the reality of the situation and don't feel betrayed by lies. Put the plate on the table in front of them and let them decide if they want to eat wants in front of them.

We have natural instinct of responsibility because we have to make whatever it is we have work and that can fall under many categories. We also have to maintain it to make it last as long as possible. And we all know that can take some work especially how complicated the world is today. The responsibilities seem endless but we still have to do it or are capable of doing it because we have it in us naturally. You just have to utilize your instinct.

The responsibility of raising a child alone seems to be one of the biggest tasks to do but those instincts supposed to kick in and get you through it. Instincts get you through anything that's in you naturally to do. Doing things instinctively like taking care of your mate and child until they are old enough to operate without you plus providing and surviving while getting along with your fellow man. There are so many responsibilities that go along with that but most time you find strength when you don't know where it's coming from. You're going to look back at times and say how did I get through that but God-given instincts. We seem to be missing out on just the main natural instincts let alone any of the other ones.

Does that mean we are too far detached from our natural state that we are forgetting about our first responsibility? You also have to be committed to the instinct of responsibility if you want to make it work for as long as possible whatever that may be. We also should be committed to being the best leader we can and making things better for others including our mate and family.

When it comes to your fellow man you should be peaceful, helpful, and compassionate towards them if you want to occupy the same space unless forced to do otherwise. You should care about what's going with someone because you might have to be helpful one day. It should matter what a person has going on in their life before you decide to do something that might harm them or their family. You should develop a concern and understanding for people so you can read their body language and tell when something is wrong.

Sometimes people won't tell you what's wrong; they leave it up to you to figure out because we have become bottled up when it comes to releasing emotion. If you are a person of concern you will probably try. Sometimes people are just waiting for a person to show concern so that they can release their emotions. Just recently I got in touch with a cousin I haven't seen or talked to since I was little.

As we were catching up and talking, she just began to cry and I could tell she had been waiting to release those emotions. She just wanted somebody to listen to her about how she had been feeling and what she had been going through due to similar family issues and not be judged from it but understood by it.

Stop judging people by what you see until you have listened to what got them to that point because you might have more empathy and understanding after you have heard their story. She also said it made her feel better and inspired probably because she didn't get judged and was able to release that emotion while being given a few incorrigible words. I became that listening ear for her.

It is good to have some of the qualities too that would probably come from the mother's genes like being gentle, pacifists, and a pleaser. I talked about being gentle but sometimes you might need to pacify a situation with your mate or child in order to be some of those other things I mentioned earlier when making them feel better or consoling them or comforting them.

Being a pleaser is just what it is, pleasing, making sure the other person is pleased with what you're doing. There should be a known enjoyment factor when attempting to put a smile on someone's face. As long as you put in maximum effort, you can be coached the rest of the way if need be.

It can be broken down in different ways, but bottom line is pleasing the other person. Those things can go a long way when dealing with the opposite sex and probably keeps the woman from having to find those qualities in other people besides yourself whether man or woman. She is normally doing everything she can to please a man because she cares and its natural but we're normally thinking about getting pleased rather than doing the pleasing.

CHAPTER SEVEN

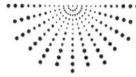

THE COMPLETE DEFINITION OF A MAN

THIS IS the total package of defining each area of your life to show that you have taken all the necessary steps to call yourself an authentic man. You have to be able to take every little lesson you learn and find a way to apply it to real life situations. Be willing to add and remove what it takes to be labeled a real man. It takes time for it all to soak in your system and become who you are in a daily basis, but as long as you have the knowledge and willing to apply it, you will become whole and complete. As long as you're not afraid to look at the man in the mirror and reflect, it won't take long to complete the process.

What we need to do is get back to our natural state of God's will and alignment. The natural state before the evils of the world corrupted every pure thought and intention of human beings. We need to get back to putting the things that were placed here for us initially, the woman, the child and the environment back as first priority and let those other things come together. It looks like we need to get back to the basics and start from point A so we can get to point Z with God guiding our footsteps along the way.

People are trying to get to point Z and starting a family before they get the basics of learning themselves and who they are and planting strong roots so you can't be moved by any and everything. You have to be equipped properly before reaching that point in life. It has to start with allowing God to be in our core foundation of learning so he can guide us on the right path and show us how to build properly, so that it stands strong and sturdy throughout the test of time.

"God wants us to mature and grow on a sure foundation." It takes time for growth to happen but you have to trust the process. You have to be patient as long as you're doing your part. If you have chosen to build something on a shaky foundation that doesn't include God then you run a high risk of it crumbling before you have a chance to make it to the top floor. "The building of a man is similar to the building of a city like Tel Aviv. Any city in Israel with the word Tel in its name indicates it was built on the ruins of another city. The archaeological meaning of 'tel' is a 'mound of accumulated ruins.'"

"What God does when building a man who dares to face him is to reveal the ruins of his life. Once those ruins are exposed, He uses them for the only thing that they are good for, the foundation of a new life."

God forces us to see what's left so we know that there's still something good there to work with. He takes all that old rubbish from the previous situation that caused you to crumble in the first place and rebuild it by shaping and molding what's left so he can build you up even stronger because now you're not starting from scratch.

"We must discover our created, God-given purpose. That becomes your goal for self-development. That discovery gives you a solid foundation on which to build. Then begin to surround yourself with people to whom you give an influential voice who have the same goal principles.

Once you learn who you are, then you can step into purpose. This should be one of your first goals as a young adult. Self-discovery and purpose. One of your early prayers in life should be to reveal your purpose so that it manifests itself in due time. This is the start of a foundation that will carry you to prominence throughout life. Then surround yourself with like-minded individuals who want the best for themselves and you. Allow it to be people you look up to so that you're always motivated.

"Obedience, commitment, and consistency lay the foundation for manhood and balanced leadership." You have to show that you're willing to obey authority figures and rules. You need to be able to follow instructions and be disciplined in that. You need to be willing to commit to something wholeheartedly regardless of circumstances, whether it be a task, a job, a person, etc. You have to be consistent in your approach to life and with your words. Your tone, your attitude and your demeanor should stay consistent throughout your day. You should not be erratic.

Don't take a stand on something then blow with the wind if it's changing direction. Be the same person at the end of the day that you were at the start. The only time you need to change up suddenly if you are wrong in your approach and you have to make an adjustment. "Your obedience starts with God and results in consistency, commitment, and what I like to call a "safe place" to dwell for those we love. It creates a structure for those we care about to be nourished and encouraged." That's the first authority figure you need to obey because his rules are first and foremost and they help you reach a level of manhood in which we want to achieve. Then you have to commit to living a certain lifestyle that shows God you can make a serious commitment before you're able to transform into the man that you were meant to be and receive the blessings that were meant for you.

If you can't sacrifice a commitment to him how will you be strong enough to make a commitment to a person who doesn't see your every move? You have to have a certain level of integrity with yourself in order to maintain that commitment. You can lie, sneak around, and cheat on a person but there's no way to do that with God. Commitment also requires you to be dependable.

"Reliability is one of the foundations for the acceptance of your authority as a man. When your word can be depended on, you will develop the influence you need in order to exercise authority. As your words become more consistent, those who depend on you will develop greater respect."

"If you are inconsistent in your obedience, your every decision will be questioned, sometimes unreasonably, because those under your authority feel no sense of security in the relationship."

"They're not necessarily questioning your authority but are the result of fear caused by your inconsistency." When you say you're going to do something, you have to follow through with it. It makes you more trustworthy and consistent so when you say it, people can hold on to it and not be disappointed. You will earn the respect of others if they know you're going to do exactly what you said or be exactly where you said you were. You also have to be consistent in your decision-making process so you're not constantly making bad decisions that are harmful to you and your loved ones.

Every decision won't be in question or second-guessed because your track record will speak for itself. They want to know if you're making the best decision for everyone involved or if you're making a mistake. You ever seen or heard about a child whose father said they were coming to pick them up and they're waiting for them in the doorway or on the steps and they don't follow through with it, imagine what that does to that child especially when it's done time and time again.

"Commitment has four key components: diligence, patience, obedience and consistency."

"Diligence means you focus on the mission at hand despite the things that come to distract you from your goals and commitments."

The only way to succeed with your vision and stay on the path is to have patience so you don't get sidetracked or inpatient because God needs certain thing to manifest within you and around you in order for you to achieve that and sometimes it can take some time. You can't get there without being diligent.

"Patience is the ability to stand in wait without panic."

"Patient endurance means possessing a calm persona while time and circumstance converge to bring about change. This characteristic in a man is a product of consistent obedience. Consistent obedience builds your ability to stand firm in unfavorable situations while you work through your problems and the problems of others."

The diligence enables you to stay focused on your path despite things that may get in your way that might throw the average person off.

"It will be easier for you to exercise patience and commitment if you have thoroughly thought through the process of what it is you are waiting for."

Allow your mind enough time to process your thoughts and think through the possible outcomes of an action and what it might take to get to the end result. It allows your mind to more at ease waiting on results.

Now these things aren't easy to achieve but you have to make a concerted conscience effort to behave in a manner that has probably been hard to do before, but you really have to have a renewed heart and a renewed mind in order to do so. You have to want to change.

"A renewed mind operates from the context of God and a new destiny rather than a negative past." When it is formed it will have you thinking differently about your future. You start thinking from a different perspective and what's important to you. First you have to be accountable and accept and admit your own faults. Own up to your role in your present situation and be willing to stand in your ruins so God may build you up again.

"He assumed total responsibility for his present situation. He positioned himself for restoration by deciding to humble himself and apologize or repent for his wrong doing."

"Once you look back and admit your failings, God can begin to build and shape the man you were meant to be."

Second, you have to want to make that change in yourself because you're tired of the outcome of your decisions.

"When he was at his lowest, he came to himself," meaning he had to internally soul-search to find the root of the problem because he had experienced his lowest point of his life and realized that he was not where he wanted to be.

Sometimes it's not until a person reaches that point and feel they can't fall any lower before they decide to change. Then they realize there is nowhere else to go but up. A different future is only possible if you are willing to change but it takes self-examination and self-reflection.

"God will give you a new sense of who you were created to be and what you are able to accomplish." When an intense reflection occurs you either run and hide or change. Most people don't like to look at the ugly truth so they turn a blind eye to the mirror but some don't like what they see and do something about it. God will give you a new feeling of life and purpose once you seek that.

Third, you have to put forth the effort towards that change once you decide to because it's not an easy thing to do but it is possible if you are willing to commit to the change. The one thing about change though is that it scares a lot of people from wanting to try it because of the fear of the unknown. Not many people are quick to travel a road not known to them, but that's where having a vision is important so that you can envision yourself doing something, so you at least have an idea of where you're headed.

Then you have to have a vision for yourself and what you want and where you're trying to go in life. You have to have the same vision for your family. You have to have the ability to see past your present circumstances to say I might be here now but I will be here when I'm done.

"Vision is the ability to see past your present into your future. Vision pulls you toward success."

"Strong vision that shapes godly character enables a man to bring order and peace to his environment. If you lack vision, you will lack structure, and this lack can lead to disorder and dysfunction." That shows you why people think and live like chaos is order because they lack vision and focus.

They're so used to living chaotic that it appears to be the way of life but if you're focused on your goal or vision it doesn't leave much room for chaos. Once your footsteps are ordered and you know what your next two, three moves are then it reduces the possibility of things getting out of your control.

"Every man is equipped to bring any situation under control, no matter how chaotic it might appear." I can walk into a chaotic 2nd grade room with kids bouncing off the wall and instantly bring order if that's your calling as a man. It can be anything chaotic, but if God orders a leader to bring calm to it, it will be done.

God sends signs to us all the time, but we disregard them or don't pay attention to them like we should. As a result, we miss out on a lot of the plans he has for us. If we are to be the leaders and teachers and visionaries that we're supposed to be then we have to let somebody give us the vision that we need to lead. And who is the only person that can place that in your spirit and soul?

After your vision, you have to be willing to be that strong leader that people can believe in because "when you cast your vision correctly, those included will began to understand your purpose in their lives and their productive participation in yours. Once your vision is well thought out and cast, you will become more secure in your personal purpose, while those around, who love and depend on you, will grow more secure in that relationship. Vision reconnects you with your innate role as a leader."

Leadership is a characteristic that is needed in every phase of your life. Now if you're not at that mature point in life, when faced with certain decisions you won't use those leadership decision-making abilities that you possess.

Men and women reveal their maturity when they handle unexpected problems with a calm and balanced approach.

"When you conduct yourself as a leader, your leadership ability will be tested in at least two ways. First, the strength of your leadership is partially revealed when you are guiding others through a crisis. More important, the strength and integrity of your leadership ability is more profoundly revealed when you are in a personal crisis yet continue to lead others effectively."

In order to have that type strength there has to be more in you than just your own will because as humans we are easily broken down by pressure because it weighs heavy on our mind. It has to be the will of God because that enables you to have the type of strength that knows God will equip you with the know-how and means to get you through the crisis.

When leading others, you have to show that can you calm yourself down in a crazy situation and still thinking clearly enough to get everyone out safely.

"Once you turn your will over to the Lord, your decisions, direction, and destiny are transformed."

You start to see more clearly, understand differently, talk differently, and move differently. We'd rather not have the pressure of failing ourselves and others. Maybe it's ok just to fail ourselves, but if we have to have somebody else depending us then it's an added pressure that we would rather avoid.

"The reluctance to lead is usually connected to your fear of rejection from a manhood perspective, along with the fear of making a mistake." That fear is usually due to our own insecurities and inabilities to actually perform as a leader because we are inadequately prepared to achieve this position.

We don't trust ourselves enough. We are worried about dropping the ball. If we fail, then we start feeling like less of a man. We start questioning ourselves and our ability to actual reach that plateau, so now you have others doubting us and us doubting ourselves. People don't understand how much that takes a toll on a man psychologically.

When Moses stood before God and heard his assignment, he faced some of those same issues of insecurities and rejection. He didn't think he was equipped to lead the people but had the faith that God had called on him to be that leader for a reason and that he would not send him in alone or unprepared.

It also shows you that in order to fulfill an assignment that you're called to do that you need direction and guidance from God every step of the way. You have to tap into that natural spirit side of ourselves that knows earth's beautiful plan is set up by design and we are part of that design.

"Men, we are wired to positively impact our surroundings and produce an encouraging expectation in others." That's why men have that ability to lead a household, pack, community, or country. There is something in our voice that demands attention. There's something in our presence that can change the atmosphere whether it be good or bad. You ever notice when talking to a child that you can tell that child to do same thing a woman of authority just told them, but they would listen and react differently to the sound of your voice.

There is a reason for that because that is your natural position in life that has been designed for you by God; to lead. If we take our rightful positions as leaders, then we can impact our surroundings and encourage those we are accountable for to produce higher results or even those we're not accountable for. It's just being an influential presence.

"Within his community, a man should be an interactive part of the solution, part of the problem-solving leadership in his community. By becoming part of the leadership, you can help bring righteousness and godly principles into that community." That statement is so true.

If you know that something is wrong in your surrounding community or household and you do nothing about it or just complain then you're more part of the problem than you think because you're doing nothing to influence change. All it takes is for a few men to put their positive ideas together to help solve a problem. As an observer, you can discern what is being done incorrectly and see clearly what needs to be done to recover. That's why no matter whether the circumstance is negative or positive, you see a man who's willing to lead the pack and other men willing to follow. It can be a sports team with a captain, a gang with a leader, armed forces with a general, or so on, there will be a person who demands the respect of others and becomes that leader.

CHAPTER EIGHT

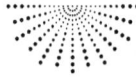

FINAL THOUGHTS

I'VE NEVER WRITTEN anything even close to a book or never seen myself as an author but when I was twenty-eight, the thoughts of a book just start pouring out of me on paper and the rest followed. The title came to me, then the right English class opened up for me to take that helped my writing technique, then an outline formed with chapter titles. A vision of a neighborhood clean-up initiative with a name and all, plus I want to do a collaboration about the book with a friend who does stage plays and so much more.

Needless to say, this all came from a person who felt lost and was searching for purpose without any vision to go off of.

"A man's discovery of his uniqueness empowers him to achieve success by the total utilization of his ability. Once you discover your uniqueness, you will understand that God has empowered you in your own special area of ability."

Once you discover and start operating in your gift that was placed in your spirit, you position yourself for success. Things tend to start opening up for you that you never thought you could achieve because you couldn't see it clearly. Your vision was blurred by obstacles and setbacks until you got clarity.

As I reflect on my own life, I can look back at my uniqueness that probably helped me get to this point that I probably considered a hinderance or setbacks at the time. But I always figured I was waiting on something big but I just didn't know what.

I was a person who was never a follower. I never followed anybody else's trends, paths, or direction if it wasn't part of my personality or what I wanted to do. Even though I might've wanted to; but it never felt right and because of that I always felt like I was supposed to be a leader. I was a person who was always hesitant to pursue anything as far as potential talents if I didn't feel that I would be great at it. I didn't want to be just an average guy doing something. You tend to get lost in shuffle of everybody else if you don't stand out. There are things that I was good at, but it never seemed good enough to me because I was waiting on greatness. This has been the only thing that I ever tried that I felt I could possibly achieve that. Not sure if it's a stretch or not but based on how I even got to this point on writing a book, I feel strongly this is a start.

Even though I'm not a person who likes or craves attention, I've always wanted to stand out at whatever I finally did, I guess like a leader would. And last, I've usually been hesitant to express my true deepest thoughts and feelings to others, maybe because I never really felt that trusting bond with many people that allowed me to open up but it was always easier for me to write it out without a problem.

So being a natural born leader, a trend setter, never wanting anything other than greatness when I pursued something and my ability to relate to anyone and a willingness to express myself through text rather than verbally are some of my unique qualities that stand out and plays a major factor in where my mindset is and what I feel I'm destined to do. Now I know they're not all a unique talent but sometimes it can be just a personality trait.

Unique is unique whether it's a physical uniqueness or a mental one, it's still your own spin to it. Either way you have to just pay attention to detail and yourself and learn a lesson in everything that happens with you, good or bad. Reflect, evaluate and analyze every situation to get what you need out of it. Figure out your uniqueness and how it can play a role in your life.

Instead of saying I'm a victim of circumstance, I finally grasped the concept of needing my background to make me stronger. You have to know where you come from and what makes you who you are in order to understand how you need to operate and conduct your actions in the future based on your genetic makeup.

"He had to come face-to-face with his past in order to move into his future." Instead of wishing your life was different as most do or running from your childhood, you have to accept the cards life has dealt you because you can't change it. You just have to see the lesson in it. Life is always going to teach you a lesson whether good or bad. Learn from it, what you did wrong, what you could have did differently to change things. It's either going to teach you what to do or what not to do.

"I really believe anything of any power that's long lasting, that's of any virtue is going to come as a result of a life-changing experience or an experience that we would consider negative, sometimes sorrowful, sometimes oppressive. I believe that that's how God develops character in us. If you can endure the hard times, the strength that develops because of those hard experiences is what's going to give you the impetus to do great things."

My experiences are what helped me learn how people felt who needed the help and what they were going through mentally. Dealing with anxiety, depression, feeling lost, unloved, unmotivated, not capable, less than are things that I hadn't always felt until I got older and realize it was more to life than just having fun. I needed to be more but without dealing with those emotions I would not ever had been able to relate or empathize with people who deal with this every day and know how bad life gets for them. I know I've never had a vision about what I would be doing or where I would be as an adult, but this was placed in my soul at this time of my life because I feel God has a plan for me to be better and to serve a bigger purpose. But it wasn't until I asked for purpose that I understood my purpose. I had to be willing to submit myself to God in order for me to become a servant while still trying to position myself to become a leader. I just know I'm taking what's being fed to me through vision and letting it lead me to where I'm supposed to be. If you do that and include those authentic qualities in dealing with your mate and children, then we have a chance to turn it around for all three parties involved and get away from this madness.

"God wants to create the real man in you-a man of responsibility, integrity, consistency, reliability and productivity." But we have to stop making excuses and at some point, become that real man. Stop letting the world around you keep you from growing into that. We have to be accountable for our own role in our demise and not afraid to change the narrative and be different from everybody else. It's in us to affect change so walk in that for the positive.

"In a world of expectation, excuses will never alter the effects of the outcome." If you're expected to do something but give a bunch of reasons why you couldn't complete the task, the result will be based on what you didn't get done not the reasons why.

"Job 1 says he is an upright man of substance and prayer, has a relationship with God, avoids doing wrong things and takes responsibility for others."

An authentic man needs to be a stand-up guy who knows he can make all things possible and acknowledges it. A man who has a conscience and knows when something is wrong and makes the right choice not to do it, mainly because he has to responsible for himself and others. He can't know it's wrong and say forget it I'm going to do it anyway knowing there would be a consequence for his action. He has to make a conscientious decision that determines the outcome of every situation.

"Many times, we men will use an excuse to distance ourselves from the responsibility of our past decisions." We feel that if we can justify why we made that bad choice, it makes it ok. We think if we run from our decisions, we can avoid the consequences. You can only run for so long and you will never duck the wrath of God. You never know when it will come back to bite you but it will eventually.

"God does not take away the consequences of our actions, and if you must face harsh or hurtful consequences, remember consequences are actually beneficial. They are designed to teach you not to repeat the same mistake again."

We have to use our intelligence and realize nothing good comes from the wrong repeated mistakes or but unfortunately most don't learn until they bump into the same wall a few times. Once you become of age there should be a certain level of common sense being used but that's not always the case.

"When I was a child, I talked like a child, I thought like a child, I reasoned like a child. When I became a man, I put childish ways behind me." (Proverbs 13:11) That is part of that growth and maturity that you are supposed to reach that makes you a man. It's your thought process and decision-making. It's your approach to situations and control over your emotions.

What will help you are the influences you are surrounded by. They say if you are the smartest person in your circle then you need a new circle.

You should be able to draw influence, motivation, and encouragement from the people you surround yourself with.

"The influence of others dictates how successful you are in fulfilling your purpose in life." Men need to get better at being in control over their environment. One of the ways to really achieve that is taking on the mind of Christ.

What I mean by that is the people in your life can have an impact on your decision-making process, whether negative or positive but you have to be guided by a whole different set of principles that are from a spiritual plane, not a physical one. You have to be able to trust that the principles that you are being led by will only point you in the right direction so that you know you're making sound decisions.

So unless a person's decision is based on that, it shouldn't be allowed to impact your decisions because you don't know their intention. People can selfishly influence you based off what they want for you or what they would do and not what God has planned for you. If need be, God will move you from the place where you are the same way he did Abraham, so that he can silence the influential voices that could sometimes be stronger to you than God's voice.

Taking on the mind of Christ could sound scary or too spiritual for most because of the fear of change but really, it's just a matter of doing things in a more conscience way. Thinking about the best outcome before you speak or perform an action and the best outcome is usually a result of a good decision. "Your conscience leads you to right decisions. It will no longer lead you into error, because you have exchanged your will for his will."

The transformation is possible only if you are willing to trade in the non-productive characteristics of your life. It means trading in your selfishness for consideration; it means allowing this new mindset to remake your personality. It means putting away that macho persona that you have lived by and becoming more accountable for yourself. This means becoming more concerned about others than yourself. You adopt a spirit of self-control and become a symbol of strength.

Another thing that can help us get past the madness is knowing your past. Knowing where you come from so you can know where you're going no matter what race you come from. Make sure you always do your research on these things whether it's through television or documented articles because there is always history of what happened before us. It helps to know the past so you can know if you have made any progress or still need to be progressing individually or as a culture.

Speaking of history, I just wanted to touch on it a little bit. Something seems to be a normal thing now but is more of a setback than people realize. The power of words can cut deep but I just want to talk about one word in particular. The word "nigga" applies here because I have heard so much about it and I think it's relevant to what I'm trying to accomplish here. I've seen shows, heard CD's and even people trying to bury the word. I just wanted to add my two cents to the subject because I'm still on both sides of the fence and understand both perspectives and I feel I can give a little insight.

The word "nigger" was used to degrade and put a race down. The term was used to make us feel inferior like our worth was nothing and we seem to start believing it along the way; or at least we start acting like we did. So whether if it's currently being used or not, if we move like our worth is nothing, makes all the difference in the world. I don't think it's about the word but the intelligence that goes with it. It's only controversial because the people who started it to degrade a race can't use the word in public anymore or the way they would like to, and we freely use the word among ourselves with a different meaning to it.

Our elders or the generations that it was used against would rather not hear it because the scars are still real in their hearts and mind. To be honest it doesn't mean much to the newer generation anymore because we know we can be more than nothing if we put our mind to it plus it wasn't used against us in that fashion, so it doesn't have the same impact. But if we walk around acting like we're worth nothing then we're right where they always wanted us to be in the first place.

Having a limited life or confined to a certain space without being able to blossom into a prominent role in society because of the power we possess inside. We as a people have the strength to builds nations from the ground up. It's a proven history fact but that power can't be controlled by others and that's scary to the powers that be.

Nothing is irrelevant and something is worth fighting for. If you feel worthless and irrelevant you might as well not be alive then. Not really but I know that's how a person can feel if they get to that point, so you do need to make yourself relevant and worth something by making a positive contribution to society or making a difference in somebody's life. Trust me it makes you feel worthy. When you bring about change in a situation, it makes you feel like you've done something because you can say I brought that about. You have to know and believe your life is worth more than nothing.

It could have something to do with the subliminal messages being fed to us through different media outlets. If you never heard of subliminal or don't know what it is, it is the hidden message behind what being said or done without being up front about it and if there's something being drilled into your psyche constantly whether straight forward or subliminally it starts to stick. It gets stuck in your self-conscience. That's why people have said, and I also feel, that the control of music or any other media outlet is a major part of that subliminal message that is constantly being fed to you.

It was realized a long time ago that music is very influential and powerful and it can reach a lot of people quickly. That's why it got ransacked with negativity because that was a way to subliminally put that image into your psyche. Like I said before about leaders, they shouldn't easily be influenced by others and are able to withstand a blow and continue moving forward. We know the negativity exists because we live with it, but we shouldn't let those images dictate who we become and what we stand for or what we want for ourselves and our family.

Even if you can't have everything you still don't have to be limited to nothing or that negative aspect of life. I wasn't trying to get too much into the racial aspect of things, but I did feel it was relevant to what I was trying to do with this project so I just wanted to give my insight and explanation from both sides of the fence. This is from a person who understands the present while still knowing the past which helps to make a better future.

We have to let go of that evil learned mindset and reform it to a place of royalty. Become part of the Royal Noir movement and take your place as kings and queens and princes and princesses of your homes and communities and beyond. Of course that's metaphorically, but that's how you should treat your home as castles. Be kings and queens, build up your castle, grow it, expand it, raise up your children to be ready to take over as royalty. Prepare them to sit on the throne as the heir and the next one to take over the family business.

"It is never God's intention to divide one child of God from another. God's ultimate aim is to produce unity."

So anybody who has an aim to divide people and families are obviously not living out the principles of God, regardless what they say they're living by. Beware of people's intent if their speech doesn't line up with their actions. Love is about bringing people together, God is love, so you know something good will come of that because the right principle is involved. Live everyday with the principles that create love, life and joy at the core of your existence and everything around you will start to give off that same energy.

ABOUT THE AUTHOR

My name is Yancey Mix. I was born and raised on the east side of Detroit and have lived there my whole life. I'm a high school graduate and a father of 4 loving children, two girls and two boys. I grew up in a single parent household until the age of 10 when I met and moved in with my father due to extenuating circumstances. I lived there until adulthood when I moved out and begin my own family.

I'm your regular hard-working blue-collar worker who loves to travel and spend time with my family. I love adventure and sports. I'm an analytical, deep thinker who's always trying to think 2-3 steps ahead. I have worked in environments around children, mentored, and volunteered in my kids' classrooms throughout my adulthood. It shed light on a subject that plagued my mind for a long time. Why are children of future not getting what they need in the world? What is happening in society?

Like a lot of men, I have struggled to figure why I couldn't get my life in order. What was I doing wrong and why? As a man have you ever wondered, what am I lacking to be like the successful men of the world? Or as a female wondered, what am I not understanding about men that keeps me choosing the wrong ones? What am I missing? Well here's more insight that may help you get those answers so that you can stop questioning yourselves and know how to fill in the blank.

www.ingramcontent.com/pod-product-compliance
Lightning Source LLC
Chambersburg PA
CBHW071416040426

LA45CB00012BA/1178